Dear Reader,

Life can be quite the wild ride, can't it? It's a mix of highs and lows, twists and turns, and sometimes, it throws us curve balls that leave us feeling shaken to the core. Trauma is one of those curveballs, hitting us when we least expect it, and it can make our world feel like it comes crashing down. But here's the thing you need to know:

Charisse has been a student and friend of mine for about 4.5 years. I have seen her overcome obstacles that seem impossible. From health issues to family and more personal things that I am not at liberty to tell, it's her story, not mine. But, I was and continue to be amazed at how well she has not only overcome these challenges, but also thrived through them and come out on top. If she can do it, so can you.

Healing from trauma is not just a possibility; it's an absolute necessity. It's about reclaiming your life, your happiness, and finding your way back to who you truly are. It's about finding strength in the places you thought were impossibly broken.

As you turn the pages of *Flipping the Iceberg*, you'll discover Charisse's own journey toward overcoming trauma and how she emerged from life's darkness. You'll find a friend who understands what you're going through and is here to guide you. This book goes beyond just healing; it's about using that healing to craft a life filled with success and deeply meaningful relationships, whether in your personal or professional world.

Trauma often leaves our relationships in a fragile state, but this book doesn't leave you hanging. It's a practical guide to not only fixing what feels completely broken, but also strengthening what remains and creating new, resilient connections.

So, take a deep breath, open the first page, and let the journey begin. *Flipping the Iceberg* is more than a book; it's your roadmap to a brighter future. It's your guide to finding joy, purpose, and the kind of relationships that light up your world once again. Your journey starts here.

Enjoy,

Krista Mashore
Krista Mashore Coaching

Flipping *the* Iceberg

Flipping *the* Iceberg

**Discovering and Celebrating
What Lies Beneath the Surface
in Your Relationships**

CHARISSE WALKER

Published by Sunshine Pages Publishing
For more information pertaining to this book and free resources, visit www.flippingtheiceberg.com

ISBN (paperback): 979-8-9906341-0-7
ISBN (ebook): 979-8-9906341-1-4

Book design and production by www.AuthorSuccess.com

Printed in the United States of America

DEDICATION

With heartfelt dedication, I present this book to my children, who have reached the age where dating and contemplating life partners have become significant pursuits. My deepest desire is that you invest the necessary time to read this book and actively engage in the suggested activities. Through these endeavors, I hope to equip you with the knowledge and wisdom to heal your trauma from divorce and bad relationships so you can foster relationships that are not only joyous, but also enduring.

May the insights within these pages serve as a guiding light on your path to finding love and companionship. May you approach each connection with authenticity, patience, and a genuine desire to understand the depths of another's being. May the lessons imparted in this book enable you to navigate the complexities of relationships, making informed decisions that lead to sustained happiness and fulfillment.

As you begin on this transformative journey, know that my unwavering support and love accompany you every step of the way. May this book be a trusted companion, guiding you toward relationships that are built on a solid foundation of mutual respect, shared values, honesty, and unwavering love.

To my husband, Gordon, who has journeyed with me on our tall iceberg. We have blazed a trail and will continue to. Thank you for your support, love, encouragement, belief, and trust in me.

With all my heart,
Your Loving Mother and Wife
Charisse Walker

Contents

Introduction

Dinner was coming along nicely when my daughter stormed into the room. She came to stand right across from me, slamming the counter with her hand. She had my attention!

Me: Hello to you, too!

Daughter: Charlie just stood me up AGAIN!

Me: What? Again?

Daughter: YES! Why does he ALWAYS do this?

Me: Do what? Act like he's committed, and then flake?

Daughter: Yes! He won't cancel with his friends, so why me? Around others he's nice, fun, and goes out of his way to make them feel important. With me, I feel forgotten, hurt, and unimportant. If people only knew the real person, they wouldn't think he was so great.

SEEING HER HEARTBROKEN AGAIN was the moment I declared my intention to write a book exploring the intricacies of relationships, drawing an analogy to the iceberg as the metaphor for their evolution. Relationships are akin to these frozen giants, where what lies beneath the surface truly defines a person. Beyond the mere glimpse of the iceberg's tip lies a hidden world unseen by the naked eye. Similarly, in relationships, we must venture beneath the facade, investing time, energy, and care in unraveling the depths of an individual to discover the beauty and complexity of a person. It is through this profound exploration that we unlock the potential for fulfillment, longevity, and triumph as we nurture our core relationships.

My desire to write this book intensified when I attained my Real Estate Divorce Specialist certification. I learned a depressing fact: In the United States alone, a staggering 1.2 million couples divorce each year, which translates to a profound 2.4 million individuals.[1] The sheer magnitude of this number struck me, because the far-reaching impact leaves an indelible mark on the lives of family, children, friends, and more.

As a divorced woman who has subsequently found love and remarried again, my heart sank upon discovering census data revealing a disheartening statistic: second marriages have a 60 percent chance of ending in divorce.[2] This knowledge greatly saddens me. Why do so many couples choose to end their marital commitment? This question echoed in my mind, urging me to delve deeper into the reasons marriages are failing. Driven by an unwavering mission, I am determined to assist as many individuals as possible in making wiser choices before entering a marriage commitment.

How do we achieve a transformative change that not only heals us but also improves marriage relations? I propose the idea of considering a person's personality as an iceberg, where a substantial portion of one's personality lies beneath the surface, concealed from casual observation. What we perceive, particularly when our interactions are fleeting, is merely what they choose to reveal. To truly know someone, we must dive deeper and swim through the layers that remain hidden; this requires a patient exploration of their depths.

How many individuals possess the certification and clearance to go on a scuba diving expedition, venturing hundreds of feet beneath the water's surface, amidst the freezing temperatures that encompass icebergs? Not many, maybe even no one. So, the question remains, how can we unravel the true essence of a person, like observing the entirety of an iceberg? The answer lies in embarking on a process I call "Flipping the Iceberg," which serves as the foundation of this book. By flipping the iceberg, we gain a clearer view of someone's personality with relative ease compared to diving below water.

Remaining true to my convictions, I wrote this book for two compelling reasons: First, to empower you, the reader, to heal from your past traumas and discover your potential. Secondly, to equip you with knowledge and tools to make informed and healthy decisions by finding out as much as possible about your potential mate before saying, "I do," ultimately laying the foundation that will lead to both happier and more enduring relationships.

Get ready to embark on this journey of profound exploration as you navigate the depths of understanding; both of ourselves and those we encounter. By flipping the iceberg, we will uncover the hidden treasures that once lay beneath the surface but are now uncovered. Let us start this climb!

PART I

I could not believe my eyes. Barbie's dark-haired Ken was standing at the podium with a microphone at the front of the room. He had perfect hair, a perfect smile, perfect cheekbones, and a very muscular build, not to mention, he was incredibly handsome. Had he not started singing, he could have easily passed as a mannequin. Added to his perfect appearance, as the piano played, he sang a song talking about how no man should be alone. Not only was he good-looking, but he was talented too!

The words faded away and my eyes had stars bugging out of them like those in a cartoon as I thought, "Hubba, Hubba!" He finished the song and sat down. I leaned over and whispered to my friend, "Who is that?" She whispered his name with a bit of annoyance. Thinking that was an odd reaction, I dismissed it and began figuring out how I was going to fly across the room to get past the crowd so I could meet him. The meeting ended and I hurried over to where I last saw him, but he was gone. I looked everywhere, but just as Cinderella disappeared at the stroke of midnight, so had he.

Months went by and I returned to college 2,100 miles away. The first Sunday at college I attended church and there he sat, at the front of the room facing the congregation. Rubbing my eyes to see if I was imagining him, nope, Ken was really sitting there! Unfortunately, I did not get to meet him that day either. After weeks of failed attempts to meet at various activities, I found out my roommates were friends with his roommates. Knowing I was interested in him, my roommates invited me to go watch a movie at his roommates' apartment. Of course I went with them! As we walked over to their apartment, excitement filled me. We walked into their darkly lit apartment and there he sat on the couch. Our stars had finally aligned.

Nine months later our wedding day arrived. We were kneeling face-to-face while the clergyman spoke. Out of nowhere, I heard a man's deep voice, as if my dad was standing next to me, whispering in my ear, "Charisse, get up and run!"

I looked around and saw no one by me. My dad was sitting in a chair across the room. Where did that voice come from? What did he mean? I looked at my parents, my grandparents, his family, my sibling…how could I get up and run? He checked all my boxes and I was so excited to be marrying him. Sure, I had hesitations, but I dismissed them and said, "Yes!"

Years progressed. We had four beautiful children, I had a successful career, and we lived in a beautiful home. On the outside, we were the perfect family, but behind the scenes, it was far from a fairytale. In addition to our constant fighting, I had serious health problems and my body was shutting down. I could not keep up with the demands of running a college and my family. After much discussion and trials, and several months of separation, our marriage ended and I was left with the entire responsibility of caring for my children, ages three to ten.

I NEVER THOUGHT I WOULD EVER BE DIVORCED. Growing up, I imagined the perfect family and me being the perfect stay-at-home mom and wife. The split was heartbreaking. However, what was even harder was watching the effects on my children for something that was not their fault, nor could they control. I knew that at their age, the divorce could have lasting and detrimental effects on their lives. The children I loved and worked so hard to protect and care for lost their safety, comfort, and security.

As someone who has personally experienced the profound impact of divorce on both immediate and extended family, my mission is to guide and support you in avoiding a similar path by providing essential skills and thoughtful questions for discussion with your partner. My aim is to empower you to truly understand your partner, aiding you in choosing the right partner from the start and fostering a lasting, fulfilling relationship.

I have spent years watching, studying, listening, interviewing, and compiling ways and strategies to help other individuals avoid the experiences and mistakes I made. With my first marriage, I was naive and unprepared. I believed that love would conquer all. Although I still believe that is possible, I add an asterisk that both people must work for enduring love.

Sadly, I am not alone in my divorce experience. Although the following statistics are lower than my real estate divorce class taught and were presented in the preface, many couples do not achieve the happy-ever-after they originally sought. In fact, the following statistics depict a much sadder truth:[3]

- Approximately 630,000 couples divorced in 2020; that is 1.26 million individuals

- Fewer couples are marrying today than pre-1990

- Remarriages have a 60 percent greater chance of divorce

- Couples with divorced friends are 75 percent more likely to divorce

- Approximately 2.3 persons per 1,000 divorce each year

Gretchen Livingston shares the detrimental statistics of unmarried parents:[4]

- 25 percent of parents with children are unmarried

- 35 percent of unmarried parents live together, up from 20 percent in 2011

- Cohabiting couples are less likely to be married or educated, and are much younger

- 20 percent of children born to a married couple and 50 percent of children born to a cohabiting couple will experience their parents' breakup by the time they turn nine

- 16 million U.S. single parents live with children eighteen years and younger

- 42 per 1,000 births are to single women

In addition, a survey conducted in 2015 found that 67 percent of adults say that children raised by a single parent is bad for society, and 48 percent said the same about unmarried couples raising children.[5] If society feels unmarried and single people are hurting society by raising kids outside of marriage, then why are more couples unwilling to marry today than ten years ago, and why is divorce so prominent? One reason is that individuals are not healing from their trauma, leading to unhealthy choices in relationships and self-sabotage. Consequently, when faced with undesirable situations, some will not commit to working through the issues, while others remain in toxic relationships they should not stay in.

Another reason is they are afraid to marry since they were victims of divorce as they witnessed their parents' split. I hope that after reading this book, couples will desire to marry, enter marriage well-prepared, deeply in love, with a clear understanding of their partner's true self, fostering a commitment to navigate challenges and ensure the success of their marriage.

Having experienced divorce and remarriage, I attest that marriage is challenging. I have learned valuable lessons from my first marriage, both positive and negative, and have carried those lessons into my second marriage. I have observed, worked with, taught, and witnessed students, employees, friends, clients, and family marry, only to see it crumble later.

Transitioning from my personal and professional insights, I have identified red flags and common pitfalls leading to relationship breakdowns, sparking my mission to equip you with a premarital roadmap for building a healthy partnership. Whether you are contemplating marriage or already in a relationship, let these insights be a catalyst for self-healing and relationship growth. Now, let us delve into the complex terrain of relationships, much like an iceberg—where what we observe on the surface is just the tip, concealing a vast, unexplored world beneath, akin to the intricate depths of an individual's being.

Welcome to *Flipping the Iceberg*, a transformative journey through the realm of relationships, where healing and awareness become the guiding light toward meaningful connections. What we choose to show people is the tip of the iceberg, approximately 10 percent that is above the water. Uncovering the other 90 percent that is below the surface is the challenge we undertake in this book.

This book is two-fold. Part I focuses on healing ourselves. Like skilled archaeologists, we start on an inward expedition, unearthing the remnants of our past, understanding our wounds, and attending to the tender parts within. Here, we embrace the power of self-reflection, self-compassion, address limiting beliefs, and discover our true potential. We discover that by nurturing and restoring ourselves, we lay a solid foundation for healthier and more fulfilling relationships.

Having triumphed over internal challenges in Part I, our journey now turns to Part II, where we assume the roles of perceptive detectives, diligently examining our potential partners to make informed decisions. Like skilled investigators, we sharpen our discernment skills, going beyond surface impressions to illuminate the concealed aspects of our mate. We navigate the intricacies of communication, delve into the details of each other's lives, establish expectations, identify potential red flags, and grasp the significance of reciprocity in a relationship.

As we embark on this journey of self-contemplation, we acquire the ability to navigate the ebbs and flows of love, intimacy, and vulnerability with resilience and grace. This section empowers us to approach potential partners with clarity, intention, a commitment to honoring our authentic selves, and fostering effective relationships.

Given that more people have climbed Mount Everest than ventured to the bottom of an iceberg, flipping the iceberg becomes an exploration journey to reveal our true nature, both within ourselves and our partners. In the pages ahead, I extend an invitation to join me on this transformative voyage of ourselves and our relationship. Whether you seek healing from past traumas, explore the complexities of love, or simply yearn for deeper connections, this book provides insights, practical tools, and heartfelt guidance to support you on your journey. Please note that the names and stories in this book are fictitious, changed, or embellished for privacy. Additionally, the pronouns him/her or he/she are used for simplicity in telling stories and making points; the gender can be easily interchanged in any situation. Finally, each chapter concludes with an "Iceberg Insights" section summarizing the lesson conveyed using the iceberg analogy.

As a former teacher, I believe that active learning is way more influential than passive learning. Therefore, I have written a workbook that accompanies this book. It includes questions to answer, exercises to work through, or topics to discuss for each chapter. Please visit www.flippingtheiceberg.com to find the workbook. I highly recommend you use it so that you can get the most out of this book. I hope that engaging in these activities in real time, will not only enhance your self-growth journey, but also bring deeper significance to your relationships, leading you to pursue greater meaning and ultimately manifest the fulfilling relationship you desire.

CHAPTER 1

Find the Iceberg

"At some point in your life, you will experience trauma, don't let it define or control you."

CHARISSE WALKER

In the dark bedroom closet, a fleeting moment of innocence unfolded. There Steven and I sat, playing together. Realizing this would be our last time together, we kissed each other goodbye. As our lips locked, our parents swung the door open and light flooded in, illuminating our innocent faces embraced in our tender kiss. At age three, it was but a playful peck, yet the shocked expressions on our parents' faces quickly transformed into biting their lips as they tried not to laugh. Our mere way of saying goodbye was met with embarrassment and confusion, wondering if we were in trouble.

THINK BACK TO YOUR FIRST INNOCENT KISS. How, at such a young age, do we know what a kiss was? From my earliest recollections, and even now, my parents exchanged gentle pecks on the lips when parting or reuniting. Witnessing my parents' daily kisses may seem insignificant, but it was a behavior I learned and replicated at a young age.

Have you ever watched a father and son walk out of a grocery store, mirroring each other's strides and facial expressions, holding their shoulders in the same manner, their bellies bulging the same way? Likewise, when conversing with a mother and daughter, you undoubtedly hear similar voice inflections and tones. Although the physical build and voice are genetic, these learned behaviors highlight how children naturally learn from their parents.

Returning to my experience with Steven, my encounter depicts the profound influence my parents had on me. Research supports that the first few years of a child's life are the most formidable of their life. From social and cognitive skills to physical and emotional growth, these early years lay the foundation for coping with school, learning, relationships, and life's challenges. If someone experiences trauma as a child, developmental and social problems occur, ultimately impacting future relationships.

American psychologist, Abraham Maslow, developed a pyramid called Maslow's Hierarchy of Needs that explains the five developmental stages we move through in life.[6]

Level One: Physiological Needs. This includes breathing, sleeping, food, and water—essential survival needs. These are most apparent with babies since these basic needs cannot be met without help. To discover the importance of Maslow's first level on humans, Philip Fisher, PhD, studied American neglected children placed in foster care and found these children had deregulated cortisol, resulting in numerous psychological disorders such as moodiness, anxiety, behavioral issues, and post-traumatic stress disorder (PTSD).[7]

Level Two: Safety. During this phase, we learn the importance of love and attention through nurturing interactions with our parents and guardians. We develop trust and learn to understand our thoughts, feelings, needs, likes, and dislikes. Through play and social interactions, we learn vital skills needed for lifelong success, such as how to communicate, socialize, move, trust, problem solve, and think, as these functions provide safety and security.[8] If we do not experience safety and security, it causes trauma and stunted maturity later in life. Although safety and security help improve cortisol levels, children who experience neglect at an early age endure lasting effects on their brains, thus impacting future relationships. If you, or someone you are dating suffered neglect at an early age, safety concerns may become an issue in your relationship.

Level Three: Love and Belonging. In this stage, we forge relationships with family and friends and pursue intimacy. Megan Gunnar, PhD, further discovered that the brains of young, neglected children have a change in their prefrontal cortex and a reduction in brain volume.[9] This results in difficulty deciphering between a stranger and a mother. Children who are starved for love willingly abandon safety to attain belonging. This tendency is evident in those who align themselves with rebellious groups. The intense desire for acceptance can drive children to yield to peer pressure, leading them to engage in harmful activities simply to fit in.

Level Four: Self-Esteem. This is the ability to develop confidence, respect of and respect by others, and achievement. This stage is segmented into two parts: (i) self-esteem, covering aspects like achievement, independence, mastery, dignity, and (ii) the yearning for recognition or respect from others, including elements like prestige and status.[10] Familial relationships and childhood friends have the greatest impact in forming self-esteem during this stage. We believe what we are told, positive or negative. If it is negative, we can improve our esteem by changing these negative beliefs. Chapter 2 further addresses mindset and how to rewire our thinking. If we have low self-esteem later in life, it is likely rooted in the lack of balance between these two segments during this stage.

Level Five: Self-Actualization. This includes morality, spontaneity, problem-solving, creativity, acceptance of facts, identifying prejudices, and making our own choices. At this level, we realize and aspire to achieve our full potential, seek personal growth, and self-fulfillment.[11] The goal of this book is to help you reach this level, if you have not already. See Figure 1 below to understand the progress we move through in the five stages to achieve self-actualization.

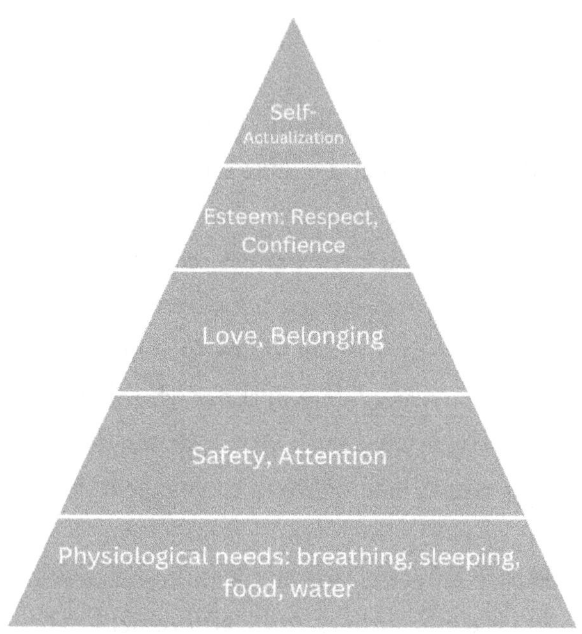

FIGURE 1: MASLOW'S HIERARCHY OF NEEDS

To cultivate healthy and enduring relationships, we must attain self-actualization by traversing the five levels of personal growth and address any lingering trauma that may hinder our progress. While this task is undoubtedly challenging, it is possible. Be patient, as the various situations and circumstances we experience cause us to move back and forth between levels.

Healing from trauma requires self-reflection and introspection to reveal hidden traumas or unresolved wounds. We do this by exploring our emotional landscape as we climb the levels of Maslow's pyramid. This is important because unresolved trauma affects our mental well-being and relationships. If the trauma is severe, it is even more detrimental to our relationships. Peace, love, and happiness can be attained through acknowledgment of the trauma and mindset work.

Picture your childhood as an iceberg. It is small when you are born, but as the years go by, your iceberg steadily accumulates from the negative encounters you face. In a secure and nurturing environment, your iceberg grows slowly, but when marked by trauma or challenging circumstances, it grows quickly. Your childhood experiences create your beliefs, expectations, and ideas, profoundly shaped by the values instilled in you by your caregivers. Your experiences determine the size of your metaphorical iceberg that you must later breakthrough to establish healthy relationships. In the upcoming examples, we delve into how childhood significantly influences future behavior and relationships, illustrating the lasting impact of our early experiences.

Tom, raised as a "latch-key kid" and subjected to bullying by his older siblings, faced a tumultuous family environment marked by constant parental and sibling fighting. To compensate for the fighting and to shield him from the financial hardships his parents experienced in their own childhoods, Tom's parents overcompensated by pampering him. He had his own car, stylish clothes, engaged in numerous extra-curricular activities his parents paid for, and had his college expenses fully covered. Tom seldom encountered consequences for his actions and was frequently bailed out, particularly financially. If he wanted anything, he usually received it without earning it.

When he married, Tom struggled to hold down a job, leading to a downward spiral of depression. Opting for his wife to be the primary breadwinner, Tom remained unfocused and unproductive. His days were spent on the computer, in bed, or watching television. When they had children, Tom stayed home, but neglected the children and home. In fact, Tom let his wife pay the bills, clean the home, and perform other parental responsibilities in addition to supporting the family. It was no surprise to many when their marriage ended. Despite surface-level perceptions of luck and prosperity due to financial security, Tom grappled with profound insecurities and a belief that he did not deserve success or love, a result of his childhood. Trapped at level four of Maslow's pyramid, he lacked the confidence to care for himself.

After his divorce, Tom moved back in with his parents and continued to struggle with employment, relying on his parents for financial and temporal support. He rarely saw his children, but was active in social groups and community events. On the surface, he was surrounded by many friends, but his relationships remained shallow and short-lived. Despite appearing socially connected, Tom endured a profound sense of loneliness, safeguarding the deeper issues within himself. His reluctance to address his vulnerabilities prevented him from establishing genuine connections, especially with his children, and prolonged a cycle of dependency on others.

Another example happened in my home, where Sundays held a special significance. Rather than venturing off to play at a friend's house, we spent time together as a family, often watching classic movies. One favorite movie of ours was *The Slipper and the Rose*.[12] It followed the familiar Cinderella storyline. The prince is coerced by his father to find a suitable bride, yet he refuses to marry someone he does not love. Thus, a grand ball is organized. Cinderella attends the ball, catches the prince's eye and they fall in love. When the clock strikes midnight, she hastily flees, leaving her shoe behind. After months of searching, they are reunited, they marry, and live happily ever after.

I watched that movie so frequently during my childhood that it served as my idealized representation of what a marriage should be like. Growing up in a sheltered environment, it was easy to embrace the notion that Prince Charming would one day appear, sweep me off my feet, and together we would ride off into the sunset. When that did not happen, I was unprepared to work through the difficulties marriage brought.

Ruminating on these two examples, I derive three valuable insights.

1. *Significant events during our childhood create beliefs and perceptions that shape us into the individuals we are today.* Tom learned from his parents that even if you fight, money buys happiness, only to find it does not buy love.

2. *We are influenced, coerced, taught, and expected to conform to certain behaviors.* Cinderella and the prince knew the importance of being true to themselves and their desires before committing to someone else.

3. *Traditions with loved ones often influence our actions.* The prince almost allowed the traditions and opinions of others to sway him from his happily ever after, but thanks to the fairy godmother, he resisted the pressures of tradition and family, ensuring he did not enter a situation he would later regret.

Unfortunately, very few, if any, of us have a fairy godmother to intervene on our behalf and ensure we make the right decisions and avoid trauma. By learning Maslow's hierarchy of needs, we can identify physical, emotional, or psychological experiences or traumas that have prevented us from progressing to the fifth level. The following five strategies provide suggestions for helping us face our traumatic feelings. Additionally, examples are included to illustrate each idea.

5 STEPS TO COPE WITH TRAUMA

1. Create a safe environment to ponder on past experiences and invest time in processing your emotions.

Identifying and then facing your trauma as well as the cause can be difficult. Take time and decide how you will approach the cause of the trauma.

Have you ever been at a family reunion and someone tells a story and you either do not remember it, or your version differs from the storyteller's? We all have different versions of our experiences, so beware of these differences when confronting your loved one or friend about past experiences, and do so with care to ensure a safe, receptive setting. Here are two examples of how your approach impacts the situation and response from the receiver:

Doug was secretly abused by his father for years. On the outside, his family was revered by others as the perfect family, but when Doug left home as a young teen, the family broke, not knowing why he left. When Doug was older, he got help, worked through his feelings, and approached his dad in a loving and caring way, showing that he wanted to move forward with forgiveness and not blame. It took his father a few weeks to talk about it, but he apologized. Doug admits that it was hard to live through, but he would not change those experiences because they made him who he is.

On the other hand, Mindy holds a lot of animosity toward her parents. Decades after she moved out, she is still hurt by them. As an adult, Mindy confronted her parents, blaming them for the decisions she made in life. Her parents thought they did the best they could with what they knew and were very hurt and surprised by Mindy's accusations and anger. Due to Mindy's approach, they still have a very strained relationship.

You may choose to confront some people, while you might let other feelings go. Before you decide to confront those who wronged you, determine your motivation for confrontation. Is it to heal, attain closure, reconcile, create awareness, or achieve forgiveness? Reflect through journaling, therapy, meditation, or another way prior to confronting them. Once you understand your motivation, express your feelings constructively, empowering yourself to maintain your emotions and avoid victimhood. Be prepared though, the receiver might not take it in a positive way, which could create more problems.

Krista Mashore constantly reminds her students that they are responsible for making the life that they want and desire. Blaming others hinders personal growth. I have been hurt by many; some I have approached and others I have let go. Some were easy to discuss or forgive, and others were more difficult. When I realized holding on to the hurt was only hurting me, it was easier to forgive. The person who wronged you does not wake up in the morning thinking about how they hurt you, so take back control over yourself and forgive others.

2. Seek support from trusted individuals, whether friends, loved ones, mentors, or professionals.

Be selective; avoid advice from those who have not experienced and overcome similar challenges. Here is an example of how taking advice from inexperienced people can be detrimental.

Depressed at twenty-one, Stan surrounded himself with the wrong crowd. Although he originally avoided drug use, he continued to attend parties where others used drugs. Seeking validation, he shared his feelings and received misguided advice and succumbed to peer pressure. Soon, he found himself out of a job and living with his girlfriend. Never thinking he would lose his virginity before marriage or try drugs, his feelings of failure and disappointment were too much for him and he did not know how to get out of his situation. Stan felt trapped, overwhelmed, and guilty. These friends offered companionship but were not the right influence or effective advisors for him.

Another example of bad advice was when I remarried. Hopeful for a smooth transition, I sought professional counseling for our blended family. During our sessions, I realized the counselor was divorced and bitter toward men, ultimately offering counterproductive advice to my family. She encouraged actions I disagreed with, especially with my daughters, spoke negatively about my husband, Gordon, and advised me to move on. I promptly ended our sessions and sought different counsel.

Licensing alone does not guarantee a good therapist. Choose your confidants carefully. Gordon and I benefited from a different therapist who remained impartial, focused on our best interests, and provided valuable strategies for our family. Finding a trained professional who offers unbiased support can be invaluable because she can provide tools for healing and growth.

3. Practice self-compassion and self-forgiveness throughout this journey. Self-criticism can be harsh; treat yourself kindly. Understand and accept yourself for who you are today and who you are striving to be. If you talked to your friends the way you talked to yourself, how many friends would you have?

I was once in a pageant. The interview question they asked was, "If you could change anything about your life, what would you change?" One contestant answered, "I wouldn't change anything because what has happened to me has made me the person I am today." This contestant won first runner-up, one large reason was because of her answer.

Your mistakes shape your journey; forgive and move forward. Isaiah 1:18 states, "Though your sins be as scarlet, they shall be as white as snow."[13] If God is willing to forgive you if you ask him, then give yourself permission to forgive yourself!

4. Incorporate healing practices that suit you. Not everyone resonates with meditation or affirmations, so find something that helps you work through your emotions.

I recall joining a company where meetings revolved around self-help book discussions and affirmations. It reminded me of the Stuart Smalley character from *Saturday Night Live* who constantly recites affirmations to himself while looking in the mirror. I thought these people were a bunch of kooks. I switched companies since I did not have time for reading and was not going to do self-affirmations, meditate, or yoga.

Fast forward a few years, and my perspective has shifted significantly. While I still do not do yoga or meditation, I do practice affirmations, read self-improvement literature and have a circle of like-minded and motivated individuals. Healing techniques abound, such as breath work, yoga, creative expression, hiking, dancing, running, weeding, and massage. Discover what resonates with you and consistently incorporate those activities into your daily routine.

5. Redefine the narrative.

Life is difficult at times, and it may feel like nothing goes our way. We can choose to be a victim or victor. Throughout my life, I have been faced with tremendous obstacles. It would be very easy to become a victim and make excuses. It would not surprise me that I am not alone in my feelings. The difference is how you handle those challenges. I now look to those challenges, often laugh, and embrace them as opportunities for growth. By turning the negative into positive, you can choose to be a better and stronger person.

Failure to incorporate self-improvement practices leaves us vulnerable to the overwhelming impact of trauma, potentially steering us away from realizing our fullest potential. I draw a parallel between life's challenges and icebergs. To illustrate the destructive nature of an iceberg, let us delve into the tragic fate of the Titanic. Considered one of the most beautiful and luxurious ships ever built, the Titanic featured a grand staircase, numerous dining saloons, a range of amenities including a swimming pool, gymnasium, Turkish bath, library, writing room, a squash court, and gorgeous private suites and cabins adorned with beautiful furniture and gorgeous artwork, even by today's standards. The Titanic was built to attract the wealthiest and most influential people of its era, earning the title the "Unsinkable Ship."

Embarking on its maiden voyage on April 11, 1912, with a scheduled arrival in New York set for April 17, 1912, the Titanic accommodated 2,224 passengers and crew.[14] Tragically, on April 14, 1912, the Titanic's encounter with an iceberg resulted in rupturing its hulls, causing multiple watertight compartments to fail, ultimately sinking the ship. This catastrophe stands as one of the most devastating maritime tragedies in history, especially since it could have been avoided.

The demise of the awe-inspiring Titanic, a vessel that captivated the public's imagination, now lying 12,500 feet beneath the water's surface can be attributed to a series of critical mishaps identified through careful review and investigation. These five pivotal factors contributed to the catastrophic outcome:

1. *Ignored Ice Warnings.* Despite receiving five iceberg warnings from five different ships, starting as early as 9 a.m. on April 14, the Titanic continued at full speed, dismissing cautionary messages.[15] Even the SS Californian sent a telegram stating it was stopping for the night due to ice, but the Titanic pressed on, leading to a fateful collision with an iceberg.

2. *Design Flaws.* Inherent flaws in the ship's construction compromised the effectiveness of its watertight compartments, allowing flooding to occur.

3. *Insufficient Lifeboats.* The Titanic carried an inadequate number of lifeboats for its passenger capacity. Due to the misguided belief that the ship was unsinkable, the lifeboats launched were only partially filled.

4. *Lack of Crew Training.* The crew lacked proper training in evacuation procedures, resulting in chaotic and uncoordinated responses during the crisis.

5. *Absence of Binoculars.* The absence of binoculars in the crow's nest hindered the crew's ability to spot the iceberg until it was too late.

The combination of these factors, from negligence to lack of preparedness, resulted in the ship sinking in a few hours, claiming the lives of approximately 1,500 passengers. Even the largest, most impressive ship broke, quite literally splitting in two. Imagine you are an iceberg, sitting in the Bering Sea near Alaska in winter. The worst storm of your life is hitting you as hard as it can, the wind is beating and chipping away at you. It is impossible to remain still in that ocean as you bob up and down.

Liken this to the worst times in your life when you felt like you metaphorically just hit your iceberg and feel like you are sinking. In other words, you feel like you cannot handle anything else. Ask yourself two questions:

1. What can I learn from my experience?
2. How can this trial help me become a new, stronger, and better version of myself?

As tough as these experiences are, if you reframe these trials to be blessings, they will make you stronger.

Here is an example of how a seemingly innocent event in my life set the stage for my future relationships. I was a few days into sixth grade and I was so excited to see all the friends I had made in fifth grade. The bell rang for recess, and I ran out to the playground. Two of my friends from the previous year were standing there. I ran up to them and asked if they wanted to play. They looked at each other, laughed, looked back at me and said, "No!"

Embarrassed and confused, I ran away to play alone. I do not recall many more recesses where I played with friends or attended parties that year. I felt isolated and excluded. Life was challenging and I developed a deep sense of shyness and self-consciousness. Sixth grade marked a turning point for me with other people. It was the year I stopped forming close relationships. Instead, I immersed myself in various activities to avoid being with other people.

Although I strived to be kind to everyone, I maintained an emotional distance, a realization made ironic by being elected student body president and earning the title, "most involved" during my senior year in high school. By engaging in numerous activities and assuming leadership roles, I realized these pursuits served as a means of controlling my surroundings and diverting my attention from the lingering effects of isolation I experienced in elementary school. It became clear that this trauma became my iceberg, impacting and submerging the potential for meaningful connections in my future relationships.

Take a moment to think back on your childhood. Identify pivotal moments in your childhood that shaped you to be who you are today. What are the traumas you experienced as a child that are holding you back from experiencing lasting relationships or your potential? Finding the iceberg within ourselves, unearthing personal trauma, and commencing on a healing journey is a courageous endeavor. By engaging in this process, you can reclaim your power, heal your wounds, and lay the foundation for healthy and fulfilling relationships. Approach your exploration with patience, self-compassion, and a commitment to self-growth. Your journey is unique, and it may come in waves, but with dedication and self-care, transformation is possible.

ICEBERG INSIGHTS

Before we fully engage in healthy relationships, set out on a journey of self-discovery and healing. Just like an iceberg, there are hidden depths within us, including unresolved trauma, that impact our connections with others. The goal of this chapter is to identify your traumatic events that have affected your mental health and relationships. We explored the process of identifying how childhood experiences influence our lives. Take the time to identify your trauma and realize the importance of beginning your journey to healing and self-empowerment. The iceberg metaphor was introduced and will be used throughout this book.

CHAPTER 2

Identify Limiting Beliefs and Mindset

**"You are the product of your thoughts.
You become what you think."**

CHARISSE WALKER

Icebergs, despite their freshwater nature, have a profound impact on our world as they break off from glaciers, ice shelves, or ice tongues. To be considered an iceberg, they must rise more than sixteen feet above seawater, measure at least one hundred feet in thickness, and cover about 5,400 square feet.[16]

DRAWING PARALLELS TO HUMAN LIFE, as children, our families serve as the glaciers from which we accumulate knowledge and beliefs. As we mature and start making independent decisions, we break free from this glacier and navigate the vast sea of life alone. During this journey, we are influenced by unseen undercurrents while weathering life's storms. We find ourselves temporarily grounded, like lonely icebergs, until humility helps us melt free, or we continue to float in the deep ocean, offering refuge to creatures above and nourishment to those below the surface.

The beauty of being an iceberg lies in the choice of what kind of iceberg we want to become. Sometimes, this journey can be challenging because we do not yet know who we want to be. When clarity emerges, our family may influence our thoughts and direction. It is during these moments that our minds, influenced by insecurities, often project thoughts that we are not good enough, smart enough, or ready for the adventures ahead.

While sitting in a Brian Buffini conference in August 2023, he invited Amanda Gore to speak about finding joy in life. She conveyed the profound insight that the sum of our experiences leading up to the age of seven intricately molds our identity, and within these formative experiences, a metaphorical malware is implanted in our brains, casting a shadow over our very essence.[17] She further explains that our essence, akin to source code, creates three core fears we all face:

1. a belief in unworthiness of love (typically if you are female), or a belief that we are inadequate or not enough (typically if you are a male);
2. a feeling of unsafety; or
3. a feeling of separation or isolation.

Recognizing that you may not have addressed your core fears, allowing negativity to impact not only your life but also others around you, sheds light on the importance of self-awareness. If you grew up in an environment where these fears were prevalent, it may become a normalized way of life. However, acknowledging that your behavior is neither normal nor acceptable creates a catalyst for change. By learning new methods to cope with these fears and seeking assistance from those willing to help, you can break free from negative situations, fostering personal growth and resilience.

The impact of these fears is profound, affecting our mindset and giving rise to limiting beliefs. In today's context, overcoming these limiting beliefs and focusing on mindset has gained significant traction, even within professional fields such as mine, where coaches prioritize mindset work before delving into specific skills. Believing in your potential for success becomes crucial, as inner doubts can hinder progress and keep you trapped in your current circumstances.

Prioritizing the development of a positive mindset before entering into a relationship is vital for several reasons. Firstly, it fosters self-awareness, enabling you to better understand your emotions, needs, and desires. Secondly, it builds emotional resilience, equipping you to navigate relationship challenges and setbacks effectively. Thirdly, a positive mindset acts as a magnet for attracting healthy relationships. Research and psychological theories consistently highlight the transformative power of mindset in shaping relationship outcomes. When you cultivate a mindset aligned with your desires and values, you are more likely to attract compatible and supportive partners. The role of mindset and its development is pivotal in laying the foundation for prosperous and fulfilling relationships.

Consider that we process 70,000 thoughts daily, with 100 billion neurons that connect at more than 500 trillion points through synapses that travel 300 miles per hour.[18] Surprisingly, 80 percent of these thoughts are negative, and 95 percent of them are repetitive.[19] Given the prevalence of negative thoughts, it is no surprise that many people struggle to find happiness. Nurturing positive thoughts is essential to cultivating a positive mindset, which is vital for successful relationships.

Think of your mind as soil; without proper nurturing, planting a seed yields nothing, but with rich and healthy soil, even a mustard seed grows into a towering bush as big as thirty feet tall. The same principle applies to personal growth and relationships. You have the power to create the person you want to be, but it starts with your mind.

Mahatma Gandhi's life illustrates the transformative power of mindset. He once grappled with anger issues and a troubled marriage. Gandhi acknowledged the power of recognizing his imperfections and the importance of self-improvement, emphasizing that all his strength emanates from understanding his limitations.[20] Gandhi prioritized daily meditation and mindset that lasted for hours. This resulted in a positive relationship with his wife and he overcame his anger. Because he overcame his limitations, he became one of the greatest visionaries of his time.

If you doubt your ability to heal your trauma, or believe you do not deserve happiness, finding the right person to have a fulfilling relationship with becomes an elusive goal. Cultivating a healthy mindset grants the ability to make purposeful decisions aligned with personal values and overall well-being.

CREATING A POSITIVE MINDSET

Unfortunately, achieving a healthy mindset requires effort. The following list provides seven suggestions to help you create a positive mindset. Visit your accompanying workbook to complete more in-depth activities:

1. Identify Your Life-Changing Moments

We all have moments that alter the outcome of our lives. Here is a story from my past that illustrates this:

During the summer after third grade, just a few weeks before school started, my parents called me into their room to tell me I was skipping fourth grade. Initially, skipping a grade seemed like a breeze, until we progressed in math and history. Suddenly, what used to come easy to me became hard. I stayed in during recess multiple times so my teacher could teach me division.

Reflecting on that experience, both socially and academically, I am amazed at how my life could have been altered had I been faced with other responses: 1) Mrs. Piper, my teacher, could have let me struggle the entire school year, eventually failing me and repeating fifth grade; 2) Mrs. Piper could have taken pity on me and passed me, even though

I did not know the material; 3) I could have believed I was stupid and would not ever get it; or 4) put in twice as much work to understand and learn the material so I was successful.

Socially, this could have changed the course of my life, including how I interacted with my peers as seen in the potential scenarios: 1) the kids could have rejected or teased me for skipping a grade; 2) they could have welcomed me and treated me like any other student; or 3) I could have acted like I was better than them for skipping a grade, thus alienating myself.

Despite the struggles, I worked harder. Fortunately, I had excellent support from my teacher and parents, and was determined to succeed. Socially, it was my best year in elementary school. The students were nice, we formed strong bonds, and I ran for school vice president and won. Because I did not let negative self-talk in, it was the best choice my parents could have made for me.

Identify one moment in elementary, junior high, or high school that impacted your life.

2. Recognize Locus of Control

This is the control you have over your circumstance versus the control you think you have.

During a crucial accreditation process for a college I helped to start up, my program director rushed into my office in distress about an issue with a vendor. I envisioned Chicken Little running through town yelling, "The sky is falling!" and laughed.[21] After the situation was handled, she asked how I stayed calm in emergencies and how I could laugh. I explained that I assess whether I can control the situation or not, and then act accordingly.

I taught this exercise to a group of young women preparing for junior high (feel free to do this activity as well). We discussed the stress they would likely face in junior high. I had them stand up, put their arms out in a "T" shape, and spin. I emphasized they had little more control over others than the space they took up spinning in a circle, so why get emotionally caught up in things they cannot control? Instead, I encouraged them to focus on what they could control, which is themselves. If things were beyond their control, I urged them to ignore or respond accordingly by not getting emotionally caught up in the situation.

After I explained this concept to my director and the young women, they realized that there is not much we can control, so if things go haywire, or are out of their locus of control, remain calm, deal with it, and move on. I was happy to see that when my director later experienced a problem, she recounted how she paused, realized her locus of control was not wide enough, and handled the problem without panicking. We received the accreditation, too!

Since we cannot control everything, we should prioritize and double down on what we can control. Wherever you focus, that is also where your energy will be. In other words, if you choose to focus on the negative in life, you will be more negative. If you choose to focus on how you are breaking rather than how abundant your life will be, then you will break. If you choose to look for the good and are grateful for your challenges, you can be happier.

When we focus on what we cannot control, this is what Tony Robbins calls the *suffering state*. This is when you feel worried, irritable, stressed, angry, resentful, doubtful, and other negative emotions. Living in a suffering state is unpleasant; it drains energy and brings sadness. Tony Robbins encourages us to aim for the *beautiful state*, where we experience positive emotions like love, happiness, peace, desire, creativity, ease, growth, appreciation, joy, gratitude, and more.[22]

Nick Santonastasso was the keynote speaker at a conference I attended. Concluding his talk, he asked three questions to move us from the suffering state to the beautiful state:[23]

1. How often do I experience emotions of anger, inadequacy, insecurity?
2. Based upon these emotions, who have I hurt?
3. Why must I commit to showing up in a beautiful state rather than a suffering state?

These are a few of the questions in your workbook that will help you escape the suffering state and move into the beautiful state. They are amazing activities that, if you take time to do, will greatly impact and encourage you to improve.

3. Realize How Your Beliefs Determine Your Outcome

Your mind projects your actions, so you must start with belief. I did not believe the importance of mindset until I hired my real estate coach, Krista Mashore. The first part of her program was all about mindset. She taught me to acknowledge my insecurities and negativities I was feeling and reframe them into positive beliefs. Unaware that I ever had a problem with mindset before, her guidance taught me the importance of positive affirmations and how they physically change the brain so that we think differently.

I developed an acronym called the "HAS" Method, which is the epitome of focusing on the positive as it reminds me to think of what I have and what I need to be grateful for. When I encounter a negative thought, I follow these three steps:

1. Halt: Stop what you are doing, immediately if possible
2. Acknowledge: Identify what you are thinking and saying
3. Shift: Turn your negative thoughts or words into positive ones

I used to feel inadequate, unworthy, and struggled with a sense of not fitting in. Shifting my focus to acknowledge my blessings, talents, gifts, and abilities redirected my mind toward positivity. Through this exercise, I realized those negative beliefs were rooted in misconceptions or falsehoods. Reframing them has retrained my brain, resulting in me being more confident, positive, happier, and successful. Learning, applying, and surrounding myself with like-minded, positive individuals led me to a tribe of people I relate to and trust. Changing beliefs has truly brought transformative outcomes.

I must thank Krista for this mind shift. Not only has she helped me, but she has helped hundreds of students and from her success has written a book called, *Stop, Snap, & Switch*[24] which discusses mindset and the importance of it.

What are some beliefs you have that have negatively determined your outcome?

4. Identify the Effects of Limiting Beliefs

Limiting beliefs and victim mentality impede success and happiness. Belief in your potential and self-accountability are key to achieving your goals. Here is an example of how limiting beliefs affect you.

As a college instructor, I witnessed the harmful impact of limiting beliefs and a negative mindset in my students. Some, coming from backgrounds where they were discouraged, lacked positive role models and struggled with self-belief. Overcoming these doubts was essential for their academic success.

I taught various subjects from first quarter to eighth quarter. I often saw students who were initially enthusiastic about their studies later doubting their ability to complete the program. Witnessing these students walk across the graduation stage with an associate or bachelor's degree in hand, transformed into confident and proud graduates, was one of the proudest moments of my job, which I looked forward to four times per year.

While many succeeded, some, like Darrell, struggled due to self-sabotage rooted in fear of success. His last class with me taught him to write his resume, conduct an interview, and compile a portfolio to show future employers. Despite my efforts, he failed his last class with me four times, causing him to fail the program and not graduate. I cannot imagine the financial consequences and discouragement he felt after two years of working for something he did not accomplish.

What are limiting beliefs that often stop you from progressing?

5. Attain Self-Actualization

The highest tier on Maslow's hierarchy of needs, achieving self-awareness can be difficult to attain, but it is possible. Here is an example of when I was not self-actualized and what happened.

Newly single, one of my first dates was with a heartthrob who saw me at an activity we both attended. I was so nervous because I did not think a guy like that would be interested in me. While driving home after the date, we talked and he asked me questions. Fearing that he would not accept me for who I was, I answered his questions the way I thought he wanted me to respond, not how I felt. It turns out his opinions matched my real opinions. When I changed my answer to his, I appeared wishy-washy. He paused, looked at me, and after a bit, ended the date. I was more worried about him liking me than being true to myself and him.

Upon reflection, I was not prepared to date and needed to work on my self-awareness first. In various situations, I was not confident to express my thoughts, feelings, and opinions, often conforming to what I thought society wanted me to be rather than asserting myself. Why would I want to be with someone who did not share my goals, opinions, values, beliefs, or interests? It became clear that understanding myself was essential to a successful relationship. I needed to learn to stand firm in my opinion without concern for differing viewpoints. This experience unveiled my areas for personal growth. I am pleased to say I have overcome this, maybe too well.

Another example of being unsure of who you are is Bill. He and Joelle had been dating for almost a year when his financial situation required him to move back in with his parents. He was unemployed, unable to pay his bills, but acting like he had a job and spoiling her on dates by taking money from his dad. Now that he could no longer hide the truth, he was concerned about how Joelle would react. When he called me asking for advice, I told him to be honest with her and let her decide how to react.

When relationships are built on lies, the relationship eventually crumbles. If someone does not accept you for who you are or what you believe, then you should not be dating. Feeling like you must be a different person to be accepted is not healthy or fair to the other person. Bill should have been honest from the beginning, but feared Joelle's reaction.

How often do you find yourself going along with someone or not being honest with someone for fear of what they might think about you? It is more important to be your authentic self than live up to someone else's perceived expectations.

6. Acquire Emotional Resilience

A healthy mindset equips you with emotional resilience, which is the ability to bounce back from setbacks and cope with challenges. Relationships inevitably encounter difficulties, but having a resilient mindset enables you to face them with strength, adaptability, and a willingness to work through conflicts constructively.

Michael Jordan faced rejection when he was cut from his high school basketball team. Driven by his love for the sport and a conviction that he surpassed his coach's perception, while in college at North Carolina, he expressed his ambitious goals. He declared his desire to be the best and would be the hardest player on the team to reach greatness. Not only did he work hard, but he encouraged his teammates to do the same, and was coachable to be successful.[25]

During his initial year with the Chicago Bulls, Jordan expressed his approach, stating that his mentality from the first day of practice was to challenge the team leader through his actions rather than his voice, given his initial lack of voice and status. Michael Jordan's commitment to giving his all is a valuable lesson for everyone, emphasizing that he does not engage in endeavors half-heartedly, as he understands that such an approach yields only half-hearted results.[26]

Jordan earned six basketball championships with Most Valuable Player Awards (MVPs). He accomplished this because of his belief in himself and his work ethic. He often worked out seven or eight hours a day, and when he was not practicing, he was watching films of the previous games. He was relentless and resilient and did not let anyone stop him. Imagine where he would be had he listened to his high school coach.[27]

Identify a challenge you have experienced or are experiencing that you feel undeserving or incapable of achieving. How could you handle it differently to create the outcome you want?

7. Believe You Can Attract Healthy Relationships

Your mindset shapes the relationships you attract. Maintaining a positive and self-assured attitude draws like-minded individuals toward you, fostering healthy connections. Positive relationships, in turn, contribute to your overall well-being. Conversely, engaging in unhealthy activities adversely affects your relationships.

In today's digitally connected world, the inundation of information has led to feelings of overwhelm and contributed to mental health issues like anxiety and depression. People often prioritize casual meetups over planned dates and opt for virtual conversations over in-person interactions. These practices have created fear of being face-to-face with someone, often unable to carry on a conversation.

Furthermore, social media has created an increased interest to pornography. Approximately 58 percent of men, though this statistic is likely higher due to underreporting or unawareness, reported engaging in watching pornography at least one time in their lives, with 27 percent within the past month. Although men are four times more likely to watch than women, 11 percent of women reported watching in the past month.[28] This widespread practice distorts one's perception of reality and creates a belief that you cannot compete or measure up.

These patterns of behavior cause individuals to settle for unhealthy relationships because they doubt their worth or the possibility of finding better mates. In some cases, the lack of experience in the "real world" results in insufficient social and behavioral skills, preventing them from attracting and appropriately responding to potential good matches. Prioritizing personal growth and recognizing your self-worth helps you avoid settling for less and acknowledging the value you bring to any relationship.

I have had conversations with numerous divorced individuals about their past marriages. Many expressed disbelief about how they allowed their spouse to mistreat them and regretted their actions. If you are not in a healthy state and are not engaged in healthy activities, it is challenging to attract a healthy relationship. It genuinely begins with your own mindset!

While your experiences differ from mine, I share my stories because I have realized I missed numerous opportunities for personal growth and meaningful connections due to allowing my past to influence my present. Without cultivating a healthy mindset and overcoming limiting beliefs, it is challenging to attain a fulfilling relationship. You might make unwise partner choices, sabotage your relationship, or unknowingly fulfill a prophecy of failure. In more severe cases, you might endure an abusive relationship, convinced that finding someone better is impossible or that you do not deserve it.

Investing time and effort in developing a healthy mindset empowers you with independence and self-reliance when approaching love, communication, and conflicts. This positive perspective not only preserves your individuality within a relationship but also prevents excessive dependency on your partner. Consequently, you can build strong, respectful, and mutually fulfilling relationships, fostering a balanced dynamic rooted in mutual support and personal growth.

ICEBERG INSIGHTS

The objectives of this chapter are to understand how your thoughts influence your actions and acquiring the ability to control your thoughts. This starts by having a genuine desire for self-healing, coupled with the belief that you deserve to have what you desire. The iceberg in this chapter is your limiting beliefs. If these beliefs are left unresolved, they will affect your future relationships. To uncover your submerged beliefs, answer the questions in the accompanying workbook to identify your traumatic moments contributing to your limiting beliefs. Next, identify your life desires and pinpoint your negative thoughts. Rather than getting stuck in your mindset, use the *HAS* Method to melt your negative belief icebergs.

CHAPTER 3

Listen to Your Intuition

"Embrace your power within by trusting your intuition—it's the key to empowerment, strength, and ultimate happiness."

CHARISSE WALKER

On a tranquil spring evening, I stood in my dimly lit bedroom, exhausted from a day of job interviews I found in the Help Wanted section of the Classified Ads of the newspaper (yes, I am that old). I had just graduated with my bachelor's degree and knew it was time to embrace adulthood and find a *real job*. My landline phone by my bedside rang and I answered with a simple, "Hello?"

Hirer: "Is this Charisse?"

Me: "Yes."

Hirer: "I wanted to offer you the position of XXX (removed for privacy). Will you accept it?"

I immediately felt sick to my stomach and heard a voice in my head say, "No, don't take it."

My intuition did not make sense, it seemed like a great opportunity. The manager seemed nice, the job seemed fun, and I could practice the skills I learned from my business minor. Despite my initial reservations and intuition, I accepted the position due to financial concerns. I hung up the phone and regret gnawed at me almost immediately. A thought came to me to call him back and decline the offer, but I ignored that feeling. Within weeks, I knew exactly why I should have said no.

THE INTERCONNECTEDNESS OF OUR GUT, HEART, AND BRAIN plays a pivotal role in shaping our responses to life's decisions. Think back to a recent significant decision you made. When seeking advice, you might have been asked what your heart or brain said, or someone advised you to "trust your gut." Recall a moment when you disregarded your intuition or inner thoughts and proceeded despite them. How did that decision turn out? Were you content with it, or do you wish you would have followed your inner guidance?

GUT

To provide context, our ancestors heavily relied on gut instincts to react to emotions like fear, anxiety, and stress. The term "gut" refers to our intestinal system; specifically, the lining housing the enteric nervous system, an intricate network of sensory, motor, and interneurons. This system regulates gastrointestinal functions such as acid levels and blood flow. It also communicates with our immune system and, astonishingly, our brain.[29]

The "gut feeling" we experience serves as a protective mechanism, alerting us to potential threats. It triggers one of five responses: fear, fight, freeze, food, or fornicate.[30] When faced with fear or confrontation, blood rushes to our limbs, preparing us for action. This phenomenon is often evident before significant events like races or performances, when athletes may feel nauseous, experience diarrhea, or sweat profusely. Hence, the importance of the phrase "trust your gut," as our body relies on gut signals to respond.

HEART

Before these signals reach our brain, they pass through our heart, which possesses its own nervous system housing over 40,000 neurons—comparable to multiple brain centers. Hence, the expression "listen to your heart."[31] These messages feed our subconscious mind, a library of experiences, thoughts, images, impressions, and feelings.[32] Our subconscious fuels our intuition, primarily guiding decisions rooted in defense or fear. On the other hand, heart-based intuition promotes personal growth and encourages expansion rather than avoidance, resulting in quicker, more informed decisions, reduced stress, and established trust.

BRAIN

Moreover, our body is physiologically connected to our brain. While our conscious brain processes roughly fifty bits of information per second, our subconscious brain processes approximately 11 million bits per second.[33] Even when our logical brain does not fully grasp the rationale behind certain decisions, our body—including the heart and gut—possesses an intrinsic intelligence linked to our emotions and choices. As we have evolved beyond a constant state of fear, we have learned to ignore, downplay, or override our gut instincts, sometimes to our detriment.

Next time you feel anxious or fearful about a decision, listen closely to your body's signals rather than solely relying on your logical thoughts. Intuition is vital, as your body processes information more swiftly than your rational mind. Recall the job decision I made at the beginning of the chapter, where my rational mind urged me to accept so I could pay my bills, while my intuition strongly advised against it? My intuition was right. Had I listened, I would not have experienced sexual harassment because I would have avoided the situation.

The ongoing battle between physical instincts and mental reasoning is a common theme in our lives. Consider a time when your intuition provided a clear answer about a decision. Did you follow it, or did you ignore it? Was your intuition correct? If you chose to ignore your intuition, did you then seek justifications for why you went against it? Subsequently, when red flags emerge, we find ways to rationalize those, as well. Persistent thoughts continue to nag at us until they eventually fade away. When we ignore our intuition, it becomes quieter.

Here is an example of how your intuition and brain coexist: Imagine, you are a freshman in high school. You get invited to a party, and you know that everyone who is anyone will be there. It is at a classmate's house you do not really know, but your friends do. Your first thought is, "I have to lie to my parents so I can go."

You immediately know this is not right, but you want to go, so you create an excuse like you are spending the night at a friend's house or going to a birthday party so your parents give you permission to go out.

You successfully deceived your parents and are now approaching the door of party house. However, an inexplicable feeling urges you not to enter. Despite this, you reassure yourself that "everything will be fine" and proceed inside. Upon entry, you immediately spot teenagers drinking alcohol, something you were taught not to do until you are of legal age. Recollections of lessons like "Just Say No" and the D.A.R.E. program from fifth grade flood your mind, and you recognize the moral dilemma. When someone offers you a cup of alcohol, you face a pivotal choice: to drink or not to drink. Regrettably, you choose to indulge, leading to an evening of intoxication and a morning filled with hangover-induced misery, accompanied by profound guilt.

While this example illustrates the physical consequences of a decision, my focus now shifts to the emotional aspect, particularly the experience of guilt. Once more, we acknowledge the physical and emotional interconnectedness of our brain, heart, and gut. When we commit an action that we feel in our heart is wrong, it affects both our emotional state and our cognitive processes. Consequently, some individuals experience depression due to self-disappointment, while others direct their anger at those offering help. There are also those who withdraw from others, justifying and perpetuating negative behaviors, such as excessive drinking, to escape the self-disappointment caused by their decisions. They might rationalize their actions by saying, "Well, I messed up, so I might as well continue."

Now apply this concept to relationships. You go on a date with someone, initially sensing that you should decline, but nonetheless proceed. Despite reservations, you enjoy the date and decide to see him again, disregarding your initial misgivings. This pattern continues over several dates, with that lingering thought resurfacing each time. You attempt to dismiss, ignore, or rationalize it away. After a while, red flags become increasingly apparent. For instance, your date displays anger and agitation over seemingly minor issues or reacts with jealousy, control, and threats when you express your desires or make independent decisions. Faced with these warning signs, you must decide whether to continue the relationship or end it.

The ability to heed your gut feelings is incredibly important. As explained before, our body knows what is best for us, but unfortunately, our minds often dismiss or downplay these instincts. The purpose of this chapter is to help you understand how your gut, heart, and brain work together so you can build the strength to listen to your gut and heart and recognize the signs your gut has been showing you all along.

Recall in Chapter 1 when I laid eyes on Ken and inquired about him to my friend, she gave a hint of annoyance in her response? My intuition registered this reaction, but my excitement and brain overshadowed it, so I did not dig deeper. On my wedding day, despite feeling nervous and hearing that voice tell me to run, my brain dismissed it by telling me I was too deeply committed. I ignored the warning signs and lacked the courage to call it off. You are never too committed to change your course and put an end to things before saying "I do!" Had I trusted my intuition, I could have spared myself a lengthy and challenging relationship.

Your intuition holds significant importance—DO NOT IGNORE IT! Your body possesses an innate sense of what is beneficial or harmful to you. Trust its signals because it discerns information more quickly than your logical mind. Sometimes the smallest details your brain rationalizes away continue to surface, but your heart and gut persist in drawing your attention to them. Listening to your intuition is a skill worth developing, even when it urges you to do something contrary to your desires. When you find yourself in a relationship you should not be in, or dating someone you know is not right, love blinds you to your intuition's wisdom.

When you begin the journey of self-awareness, mastering the art of listening to your gut or intuition can spare you from wasting energy on the wrong path. When those feelings or thoughts arise, pay attention to them, resist rationalizing, and act accordingly. If something urges you to flee, do not hesitate, use your faith, and be courageous to act!

Additionally, consider the input of your family and friends, as they, too, possess intuition and a different perspective that you might currently be blinded to. Below is one example that illustrates the importance of listening to your loved ones and using their insight:

From ages thirteen to seventeen, I attended an annual girls camp. The fourth year included an overnight hike that all the girls looked forward to. My parents, who led the hike, kept its details secret and had all previous year girls swear to secrecy. At sixteen, it was finally my turn to go. During the hike, I suggested a shortcut, taking a dry creek bed instead of the winding switchback trail. Initially, my dad, who was experienced on the hike, refused my idea. However, I persisted, and he eventually allowed me and a few others to take the creek bed route while he guided the rest. Thirty minutes later, we saw my dad and the others at the mountain's summit, still waiting for us. Our path was much more challenging and time-consuming. When we finally reached the group, my dad extended his hand to help me up and asked, "Are you ready to listen to me now?"

My dad's previous experience taught him the best route and what to avoid, but I doubted him and thought I knew better. Sometimes our loved ones provide valuable insights regarding our relationship based upon wisdom and experience. Instead of listening to them, we choose to ignore their advice, thinking we know what is best for us, or the right approach. Sometimes, our inner voice offers clear guidance; yet, like that stubborn sixteen-year-old, we choose our own path. How often have your friends, family, or your initial feelings been wrong when it comes to your relationships? Take time to ponder your feedback and listen clearly.

WHY INTUITION IS GOOD

Following your intuition, or inner voice, provides valuable insight and guidance when facing situations that involve the need for the following eight activities:

1. Creative Problem Solving

As stated previously, our brain processes so much information that our brain filters out what it thinks we want to know, often leading to bias, especially if we are used to anxiety, negativity, or fear. Fortunately, our intuition processes these emotions as well and creates alternative ideas our logical brain might not provide.

2. Quick Decision Making

Decisions use logic or intuition. Sometimes we analyze a decision into what I call decision analysis paralysis, meaning we do not decide because we have too many facts or choices. By following our intuition, it speeds up the decision-making process without overthinking.

3. Emotional Awareness

Intuition helps us tap into our emotions and feelings, enabling us to better understand our needs, desires, and motivations.

4. Navigating Ambiguity

In situations with incomplete information or uncertainty, intuition helps us navigate and make sense of complex situations.

5. Trust and Authenticity

Following our intuition leads to choices that align with our authentic self, helping us make decisions that resonate with our values and true desires.

6. Relationships

Intuition plays a role in understanding the emotions and intentions of others. It helps us pick up on nonverbal cues and assess the dynamics in relationships.

7. Risk Assessment

Intuition provides a gut feeling about potential risks or dangers that might not be immediately apparent, aiding in our safety and well-being.

8. Alignment with Goals

Intuition guides us towards decisions that are aligned with our long-term goals, helping us make choices that contribute to our overall well-being and success.

At some point in your relationship, it is likely that you will be faced with one or all eight of these situations, so learning to follow your intuition is critical. With any new skill, practice is key. Whether it be to not listen to a song, watching a movie, driving on a certain road, calling a person who popped in your head, or saying something you are too afraid to say, do it! Learning to differentiate between genuine intuitive insights and fleeting emotions or biases is a skill that protects you from situations you could later regret.

There are multiple times I did listen to that inner voice and I had incredibly positive experiences. I can also recite multiple times I wish I would have listened and did not. Reflecting on these experiences, I cannot think of one time where I regretted following my inner voice. Had I listened to my intuition more throughout my life, I would have saved myself tons of heartache, years of mental and emotional pain, and so much money! That voice will get louder, and it will get easier to follow the more you listen.

ICEBERG INSIGHTS

This chapter focuses on the importance of intuition as our guiding rock. That rock in this chapter is our iceberg. Learn to listen and this can be your good iceberg. Your intuition is the substantial mass beneath the surface, providing direction, even when the reasons are unclear (the 10 percent visible above the surface). Rely on your rock, and it will guide you to where you should go, even in situations where the *why* may remain elusive. The power lies in acknowledging and trusting your intuition for profound understanding and meaningful decisions.

CHAPTER 4

Withstand the Pressure, Push Back

"Peer pressure and social norms can influence actions, but acknowledging them as excuses is the path to reclaiming personal control."

CHARISSE WALKER

I taught sociology at a technical college where students, mostly males, attended four hours per day, five days per week, for two years. Teaching this class was a rewarding experience because it delved into subjects like cultures, race, socioeconomic class distinctions (including upper, medium, and lower income levels), and various other aspects of social interaction. When students enrolled in my class, they had already spent a year together, fostering strong bonds, camaraderie, and freely expressing their opinions. They frequently teased, joked, and collaborated with each other. I emphasize this to underline their comfort with one another, enabling them to provide candid feedback, challenge one another's ideas, and hold each other accountable. During one lesson centered on social interaction, I initiated an experiment about an hour into the class. I divided the class into two groups: the "informed students" and the "test student." To prepare my informed students for the experiment, I sent the test student on an errand, explaining the activity to the informed students in his absence.

I held up Paper 1 that had lines A, B, and C on them. I held up Paper 2 that had line D and asked which line D matched, A, B, or C? I had three different versions of Paper 2 where Line D matched with A, B, or C. I instructed them that the first four times I held up Paper 1 and 2, I wanted them to give the correct answer, and then when turn five started, I wanted them to give the wrong answer. The informed students were told to copy the answer of the first person I called on, no matter what. Below is an example of the pictures I used.

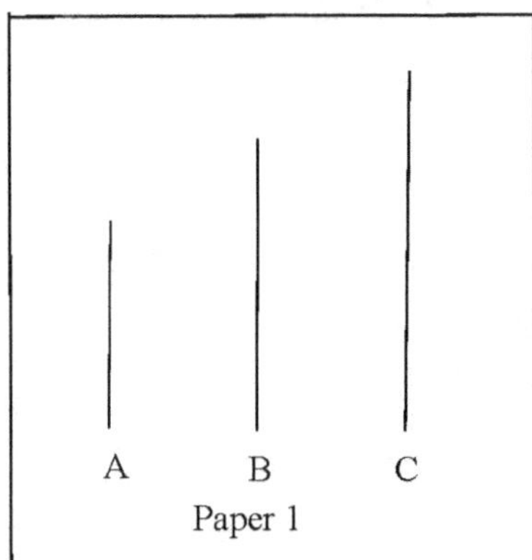

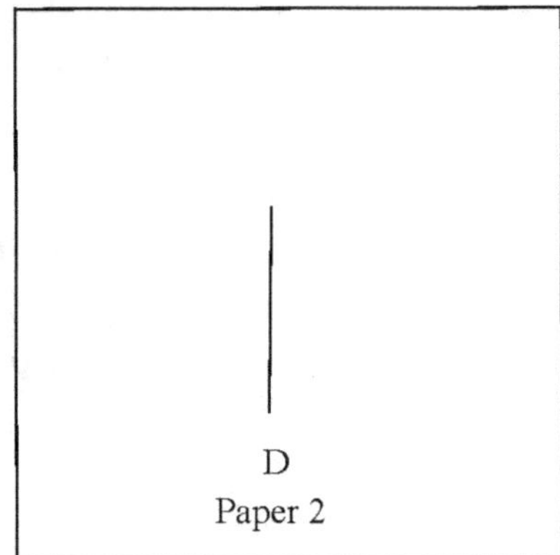

When the test student reentered the room, I continued teaching the lesson. I then moved on to a new topic, which was the experiment. I asked the class to tell me which line D matched with, A, B, or C. During the first four turns of holding different sizes of line D up, the informed students all answered correctly. I randomly called on different students, including the test student, to go first to gain his trust. By the fifth turn, the informed students gave the incorrect answer and all the informed students followed. When I asked the test student, he looked at the paper, paused, looked again, squinted his eyes, looked at the other students, and then matched the students' incorrect answers. I repeated this exercise two to three more times and the test student matched the incorrect answer almost every time.

I taught this class repeatedly for nearly five years, altering the personality type of the test student. Whether he was outspoken, reserved, the newcomer, or the leader, on almost every occasion, the test student followed the lead of the informed students, even when the answer was incorrect.

Following the experiment, we debriefed, and I asked the student why he chose the wrong answer. The most common answer the test student gave for copying the wrong answer was that he questioned his own judgment or did not want to be different. Occasionally, I saw some students follow the incorrect answer, and then give the right answer a few rounds later, figuring that something was up.

THIS EXPERIMENT SHOWED THE IMPACT of peer pressure. People do not often feel confident and comfortable enough with themselves, so they end up going along with the group. Think of a time in your life when you found yourself doing, saying, or not saying things you knew you probably should have for fear of the reaction of others. Additionally, have you ever been in a class where you want to ask a question for clarification, but were afraid to raise your hand for fear of looking stupid, so you remain in confusion instead?

Studies show that peer pressure has both positive and negative effects on teens. Since only about 80 percent of a teenager's brain is developed, teens struggle to make good decisions, resulting in skipping school, behaving badly, trying drugs or alcohol, and rebelling against their parents.[34]

INFLUENCE OF ADOLESCENCE

Until approximately the age of eighteen, we are nurtured in a state of dependency, leaning on the guidance of our guardians, often our parents. In these formative years, their counsel becomes our compass, shaping our decisions and aiding in the exploration of our identity. This period serves as a practice ground, a journey where we mold the essence of our aspirations and self-discovery. Approaching adulthood, the expectation is that we have reached the pinnacle of Maslow's pyramid, securing a robust emotional foundation. Yet, reality often finds us reliant on external sources for entertainment, comfort, and validation.

Our screens entertain, relationships comfort, and authoritative figures reassure us, becoming crutches in our journey. Graduating from the protective cocoon of adolescence without ascending to Maslow's fifth level can lead to decision-making struggles in our twenties and beyond, marked by impressionability and complacency in the pursuit of acceptance. The crucial task lies in cultivating a deep understanding of oneself, establishing core values, beliefs, morals, independence, confidence, and a comfort with solitude during these formative years. This foundation becomes our guiding compass through life's complexities, fostering sound decisions and a resilient sense of self.

ESTABLISH SOLIDARITY

Jay Shetty deciphers the difference between loneliness and solidarity in his book, *8 Rules of Love*.[35] He states that loneliness affects our ability to make positive decisions regarding relationships, while solidarity encourages people to develop self-confidence and self-trust. He suggests doing a solo audit where people do certain activities by themselves and then track how it made them feel.

If you become comfortable doing things on your own, then you will be stronger to withstand the peer pressure that my class experiment demonstrated. Shetty suggests learning a musical instrument, going to a museum, seeing a movie, or eating out by yourself because it forces you to spend time alone. By doing these activities, you get comfortable spending time by yourself and become friends with yourself first. When you are comfortable being alone, he proved that it raises your self-esteem, resulting in healthier relationships later.

Shetty further states that when you learn to rely on yourself, then this solidarity will help you improve your senses. If you do not become comfortable on your own, then love leads to blindness because you experience sensory overload. When you become happy with solitude rather than isolation, you can withstand the pressure a relationship brings.

Now that my children are getting older and moving out, I continually remind them of two actions:

1. Decide your own morals, values, and priorities. Become comfortable enough with yourself and your decisions so you can stand up for yourself when situations arise. My bigger hope is you avoid the situations you know you should not be in altogether so you do not succumb to peer pressure when you encounter uncomfortable situations.

2. Surround yourself with champions. The reason is that your friends wield considerable influence, commanding your attention, time, and ultimately shaping your beliefs, attitudes, behaviors, and even your appearance.

In *The Compound Effect*, Daren Hardy emphasizes that the people we consistently associate with can determine up to 95 percent of our success or failure in life.[36] If we surround ourselves with negative influences, we risk adopting those traits. On the contrary, being in the company of positive individuals striving for improvement can serve as motivation to do better. Jim Rohn's wisdom highlights this idea, expressing that you are shaped by the five individuals you spend the most time with.[37]

As youth or those struggling with self-esteem, rebellion, or a desire for acceptance, it is common for individuals to associate with a crowd their loved ones disapprove of, often leading to poor choices. I hope I have emphasized the importance of choosing morally uplifting people so you avoid the negative impact of people who are not positive or motivated to improve their lives. By doing this it could help prevent you from falling into bad habits.

Cornelia Horton serves as a great example of someone who defied societal pressure by prioritizing self-reflection at the age of thirty, despite pressure to marry at a young age like her younger sisters. While facing disapproval from her mother, she challenged the notion that marriage defined a woman's life. Enrolling in a stenography class, her teacher recognized her business potential, leading to an interview with Mr. Gimble. Impressed by her determination, he hired her, but she kept her success a secret from her family since women working at that time was uncommon. Eventually, she revealed her achievements and surprised her family with the unexpected marriage to Mr. Gimble.

The 1918 story of Cornelia Horton challenges societal norms that labeled her an old maid at thirty for being unmarried. Her inspiring journey showcases her self-assurance and resilience against societal pressures, opening doors for employment in an era when few women worked. Rejecting the idea that marriage defined a woman's purpose, Cornelia's authentic path led to an unexpected love that mirrored her strength of character.

This tale reminds us that embracing personal agency and resisting external pressures can lead to genuine connections and love on our own terms. Cornelia's example highlights the power of staying true to yourself, even in the face of societal expectations. Much like her, finding contentment independently can often lead to unexpected love. The satisfaction was even sweeter when Cornelia's sisters ran into their mother's home, looking disheveled, and shouted, "Mamma, mamma—Cornelia, the old maid—she has out-married us all!"[38]

Taking the time to push away societal and familial pressures to find who you truly are and decide what you want helps grow your confidence, ultimately accomplishing what you desire. I have not only witnessed it happen with others but also experienced it myself. It is a wonderful feeling to acquire strength of character and confidence that other people's opinions no longer sway you to act or believe a certain way, resulting in incredible freedom.

ICEBERG INSIGHTS

Succumbing to peer pressure due to lack of confidence or inadequacy can push you into decisions you would not normally choose. The iceberg in this chapter involves identifying what social pressures you are facing from friends, family, work, church, and any other social groups so you can become stronger and empower yourself to build resilience so you can withstand the influences you are experiencing. The next iceberg to climb is withstanding the pressure of those you are dating. If you are not interested in him, be honest and do not feel pressured to date or engage in any activities you are not comfortable or ready for.

CHAPTER 5

Believe In and Act On Your Potential

"Unlocking our potential relies on continuous effort and belief, not inherent strength or intelligence."

Charisse Walker

Sitting in a freshman college class, my teacher stood up and said, "It is time to write your eulogy!" Suffering from severe chronic fatigue and multiple complications as a result, feeling alone, and unable to call my parents for solace since it was a long-distance call—the ancient days when cell phones did not exist and long-distance calls cost money—this was the last thing I wanted to do. The assignment required me to imagine who would attend my funeral, who would speak, what they would say, and what songs they would sing. I also had to write what my kids would say. I was seventeen!

HESITANTLY, I WROTE OUT MY FUNERAL. I described what I wanted family members to say, the legacy I wanted to leave with my family, and the impact I wanted to have on the world. Tears streamed down my face as I completed the assignment. Years later, I repeated this exercise at a seminar. My tears were even bigger as I envisioned my funeral, with my six children in attendance and what I hoped they would say. If done in the right mind frame and you take the time to ponder, this exercise is life-changing because it provides the roadmap of how you want to live your life. It also identifies your priorities and the life you want to live.

Having a direction for your life is important. Numerous studies have been conducted where they blindfolded the subjects, placed them in a forest or desert, and told them to walk in a straight line. No matter the setting, the subject walked in small circles.[39] Similarly, without a plan in life, we wander, not ever progressing forward. That is why setting goals, both small and large ones, are important, because they direct our daily choices.

In the *12 Week Year*, Brian Moran and Michael Lennington state the importance of breaking down your goals into small pieces and focusing on only a few at a time.[40] Then, you make a month become a year and a day become a week. If you do this, you end up accomplishing more than you would in a year. Another technique to use each day is called the Pomodoro technique, where you set up twenty-five-minute uninterrupted intervals four times a day, taking a two-to-five-minute-break in between, and a fifteen-minute break at the end of the cycle.[41] It is estimated that you create sixteen more productive hours in a week by using this method. By having specific goals and a plan with action steps, provides hope, purpose, and motivation for a better future.

DREAM, BELIEVE, DARE, DO

A prime example of embracing purpose and realizing your potential is embodied by Walter Elias Disney, known as Walt Disney.

From age seven, his entrepreneurial and artistic spirit was seen as he sold his drawings to neighbors. Following military service and stints with various magazine and newspaper companies, he co-founded Iwerks-Disney Commercial Artists, which failed two years later. Undeterred, he created Laugh-O-Grams, which also went bankrupt.

At the age of twenty-two, with only $40 in his pocket, a caricature sketch, and a few belongings, he headed to Hollywood, California. He set up shop in his uncle's garage and joined forces with his brother, forming Disney Brothers Cartoon Studio, and then Walt Disney Studio. Unfortunately, a dispute and separation with his distributor left Walt to once again start over. As a result, he developed the now-famous Mickey Mouse in 1927, thus paving the way for his future success.[42]

Navigating through two world wars, economic depression, and the decline of rival amusement parks, Walt conceptualized an amusement park unlike anything in the world. Despite financial setbacks, he embraced a new medium—television—to raise funds to help pay for the construction of his park. Ignoring the many naysayers and pushing through the constant obstacles he encountered. He drew from his childhood memories, experiences, and ideas to create a wonderful place for both adults and children to enjoy, and employed "imagineers" to bring his vision to life. His dream became a reality when Disneyland opened on July 17, 1955. Ironically, it became known as "Black Sunday" due to the numerous challenges that happened on opening day.[43]

Undeterred by his initial hurdles, Walt Disney turned adversity into opportunity. He learned from problems he encountered and continued to push on because he had a vision and knew the potential of his vision. The original $17 million cost to build his park became an overnight success, resulting in the creation of twelve Disney theme parks located throughout the world, and a large portfolio that is now worth over $166 billion, as of December 2023.[44]

Guided by his powerful motto "Dream, Believe, Dare, Do," Walt Disney created happiness for billions of people on earth.[45] He could have given up multiple times, yet due to his unwavering vision, belief, passion, and commitment, Walt confronted adversities, consistently pushing forward. By transforming imaginative ideas into tangible realities, he fearlessly embraced the act of dreaming big, daring to take risks, and taking decisive actions. In doing so, Walt blazed a trail few have ventured upon, and has changed the world as a result.

Disney's path was not easy. He faced numerous setbacks and I am sure he questioned his potential and vision, but he persevered. Before you ever make a difference for someone else, you first need to make a difference with yourself.

You can accomplish this in five ways:

1. Believe.

You must believe that you are just as good as anyone else and that you can accomplish what they can. When you listen to people's success stories, many of them will tell you they were bankrupt, homeless, lost hundreds of thousands of dollars, or tried 167 different ideas before the ONE idea took off.

2. Think of someone successful you admire.

Do you believe you can be like that person and have what that person has or build what they have built? That person is no different from you, other than they took action to achieve their desires and you may not have, yet. It is time to put away your fears and walk into your bright future. Embrace it, be willing to alter the destination, but do not move forward without a direction or you will end up going in circles like the subjects did in the blindfold experiment. It will not be easy, but with hard work and dedication, you will find success.

3. Allow yourself to be led.

At times you may feel directionless, lost, or going in the wrong direction, but if you follow your intuition and trust in God, then you will be led to where you are supposed to be. Like Walt Disney, you must take an active role in your life by envisioning, acting, and continually progressing forward, despite your challenges.

If you are struggling with knowing your purpose or feeling insignificant, that is normal. This is often because we have allowed our previous traumas to shape our future. What if I told you that instead of allowing our past to shape our future, we allow our present circumstances to shape our past perceptions, and our envisioned future to shape our current perspective? Confused? That is how I felt while sitting in a seminar where Dr. Benjamin Hardy spoke. He implied that when we aspire to achieve what seems insurmountable in the future, it becomes the filter through which we view the present. He also suggests that in pursuing our future goals, 80 percent of our present situation is a distraction. Instead, we should focus on the remaining 20 percent and then set outrageous goals that encourage us to push ourselves, resulting in ten-times the growth.[46]

For instance, my goal is to run a marathon in six months. Despite a recent surgery that left me on bed rest for four weeks, several hip surgeries, needing a hip replacement resulting in continued pain, and permanent foot damage from broken feet, the prospect of completing a marathon appears nearly impossible. However, my determination remains unwavering, and I am committed to achieving this goal, regardless of any medical advice or familial beliefs to the contrary.

To accomplish my goal, I need to remove the 80 percent (my distractions) and focus on the 20 percent. This means that I need to focus on the 20 percent of my life I am doing right. Yes, I am drinking two cups of water, so now I need to increase my intake to eight. I am getting four to six hours of sleep, now I focus on going to bed earlier. I am getting 6,000 steps per day, so now I need to focus on getting 10,000 steps. I need to create an exercise and meal plan so I eat better and have the muscle and energy to run for long periods. By focusing on these good habits and envisioning passing the finish line, I will accomplish my goal.

Thus, we can achieve whatever we want in life because we are the only ones standing in our way. There are things in my life that I know I am supposed to accomplish and feel called to do. Lately, I cannot stop thinking about those things because I want to impact and help others realize their potential.

This fire came when I started teaching college and is one of the motivators for me to write this book. If you allow yourself to listen to others who are negative and keep you down, you are missing out on the opportunity to reach your full potential. By not following through on what I feel called to do, I am being selfish because I am not serving and helping the people I am meant to; the same goes for you.

Take a minute to think back to when you were a child and remember who you wanted to be when you grew up. Now remember when you were a teenager, who did you want to be? Did that answer change? Fast forward to today, has your answer changed? Are you who you wanted to be? Are you who you want to be now? If not, who or what is holding you back?

4. Find your champions.

Frequently, you might encounter resistance from a family member or partner who, out of guilt for their own actions or inactions, opposes your pursuit of success. A poignant illustration of this occurred when I decided to pursue my master's degree. I had given birth to my third child and resumed my full-time job after my maternity leave. Within a week of returning to work, my manager summoned me to his office. He informed me that by the end of the quarter, I would no longer be teaching because I did not have my master's degree, citing accreditation requirements. Despite receiving the Instructor of the Year award and consistent high praise from my students and colleagues over the years, I was in jeopardy of losing my job.

Fortunately, I was grandfathered into the position; however, I refused to let this be the sole reason for retaining my job and promptly enrolled in a twenty-four-month graduate program which started the next month. When Cassandra, a close family member, found out I started my graduate program, she initiated a barrage of guilt trips, accusing me of selfishness and neglecting my three children who needed their mother. For eight months, I frequently heard statements like, "Why do you feel the need to pursue a degree? You already have a job; there is no necessity to undertake this now," or, "Your kids need you, you're being selfish."

I worked twelve-hour days three days per week so I could complete my schoolwork and be home for my kids the rest of the time. Juggling motherhood, my job, and schooling became difficult, especially while nursing a newborn and caring for three-year-old twins. I barely slept and the guilt was unbearable at times. To finish my program sooner, I doubled up and finished in fifteen months, now requiring forty hours of homework and up to fifty hours of work that included teaching, preparing, and grading papers.

Reflecting on that time, I do not know how I got through it, but I did. I am so grateful I committed to what I believed I was supposed to do, and that belief, also known as my why, drove me to manage the difficult load I was carrying and accomplish my goal. Unaware at the time, this degree saved me financially. I became the Dean of a different college before finishing my schooling, and shortly thereafter ended up opening a college. Had I not had my degree, I would not have received that opportunity, which doubled my income. In addition, a few years later I became a single mother. Both my life and my family's lives were blessed because I listened to my intuition, knew my potential, prepared for my future in the present, and ignored the naysayers.

I do not remember the stress or papers I wrote, but I do remember the hurtful things Cassandra repeatedly said to me. Had I listened to her, my life would be much different today; most likely filled with regret. It was likely that Cassandra was dealing with her own demons and regrets and subconsciously trying to prevent me from being successful so she could feel better about herself.

This is one reason why it is so important to surround yourself champions who support you, especially when you have dreams and goals you want to accomplish and they have not followed through on theirs. Unfortunately, I have distanced myself from people I used to spend time with because they are negative and embrace the victim mentality. This negatively can discourage you and bring you down, so surround yourself with cheerleaders so you can remain focused on your goal and achieve your potential.

5. Find your purpose.

If you do not already know your purpose or desire, take time to ponder and figure it out. If you are feeling down, believe that you can have what you want, you can accomplish what you desire, and you are meant to do more. If you are still trying to figure out what you should do. Start with what you believe and desire now. Like many before you, you will be directed to where you should be.

ICEBERG INSIGHTS

In our journey through life, each of us possesses a distinct purpose and innate talents specifically tailored to fulfill that purpose. The analogy of the iceberg in this chapter underscores the importance of concentrating on the visible 10 percent above the surface, representing our apparent abilities, and proactively improving these talents. As you develop these talents and pursue these visible skills, the remaining 90 percent beneath the surface—representing hidden potential—becomes exposed. By exploring and nurturing this untapped reservoir of capabilities, you not only enhance your personal growth but also pave the way to fulfill your ultimate purpose and fully embrace the entirety of your destined self.

CHAPTER 6

Discover Your Intention

"What you mean when you do something really matters. Your intentions shape your outcome and the world around you."

Charisse Walker

Sitting in a semicircle of a small room with several other young teenage girls, our teacher taught us a lesson on recognizing the significance of identifying qualities in a potential spouse. She then handed us a three-by-five notecard and pen and told us to write down the characteristics we desired in our future husband. Being in high school, I thought this was a little weird since we were so young, but did the activity anyway. A few characteristics quickly rolled from my mind and onto the notecard, and soon the notecard was full. The teacher told us to carry that list with us, adding to or taking away from it as the years and our relationships passed. The purpose was to identify characteristics we wanted in a spouse so we do not settle when we are older.

I CARRIED THAT NOTECARD IN MY PURSE throughout high school and even into college. Periodically, I referred to it and did exactly as my teacher suggested, adding to and removing qualities and characteristics as I matured and experienced the good and bad of young love. As the card filled up, I made mental notes of what I did and did not want in a partner.

The summer after my freshman year of college I moved home, and that is when I saw my future husband. Recall my story in the Preface in Part 1 about seeing Ken for the first time. My Ken checked almost every characteristic on my notecard and in my head. Thinking I was marrying my ideal husband, based on my well-worn notecard, everything seemed perfect. Until the third day of our honeymoon, when we experienced our first fight. Less than one month later, while driving back to college and bickering over silly things, I remember saying, "Oh, we have such a great marriage!"

The only measure I had of the quality of our relationship was watching *The Slipper and the Rose*, my favorite childhood movie. I expected Prince Charming to sweep me off my feet and for us to have our happy-ever-after, which to me meant no fighting. Since I did not see my parents fight, I did not know that disagreements were normal, especially as we discovered more about each other.

Ken was brought up differently from how I was raised, so we needed to learn how to communicate and work through our differences. Unfortunately, the more we uncovered about each other, the more we realized we were too different, and after fifteen years, we divorced. Many reasons led our relationship's demise, and it was not due to our little fights. Trying to work through the marriage and then having it end in divorce was the most difficult event I experienced up to that point.

For this reason, one of my own goals and intentions for writing this book is to minimize divorce and maximize marital happiness among couples. After experiencing, studying, and teaching numerous classes about relationships over almost three decades, I have realized that lack of intention is a contributing factor to divorce.

STEPS TO INTENTION

The following is a five-step process to incorporating intention into your life and relationship.

1. Identify Your Intention

While single after my marriage, I studied the experiences of other single parents by observing, learning, and conducting interviews. Additionally, I actively engaged with the narratives of my nearly 5,500 students, hundreds of employees, neighbors, church members, and friends. These individuals shared stories of their childhood traumas, idealized relationships, and heartbreaking or shocking breakups. Having navigated through the various relationship stages with myself and those I just listed, I have witnessed countless relationships evolve from budding love to busting with disdain. I have seen so many God-fearing couples transition from initial stages of love and happiness to eventual disintegration of the marriage marked by sorrow, anger, pain, and rejection of God. The perplexing question is, how do relationships that once thrived in love end up in divorce mere months or years later?

In my first marriage, we embarked on a symbolic hike ill-equipped for the journey ahead. Essentially, our metaphorical backpacks contained nothing more than a water bottle and a compass, lacking essential provisions such as food, emergency kits, a guide, and clothing. While we aspired to make our marriage thrive, our actions and preparations did not align with the requirements to manifest our shared vision. We lacked a roadmap to guide our marriage toward a specific destination or intention. Despite aiming for an enduring marriage, our failure to actively work towards it resulted in losing sight of our initial intention.

According to Newport Academy's Chief Experience Officer, Kristin Wilson, setting intentions lays the foundation for growth and change, as it signifies a conscious choice to focus on something we value.[47] In a relationship, if you have no intention, you lose sight of what you are working towards. My ex-husband and I lacked intention, resulting in our divorce. If you want to make positive changes in your life, identify your intentions.

2. Set Your Intentions

What is preventing you from healing and taking action to improve yourself? Is it fear, trauma, insecurity, or something else that is stopping you? Knowing who you want to be, what you believe, how you want to live, and being honest about whether you are happy in your current situation or not are the first steps to improving your life.

If you want to find Mr. or Mrs. Right, what do you need to change within yourself to be ready for him or her? If you do not identify what you want and live up to your expectations, what do you think the results of your future relationships will be? What are your goals for your life? If you do not have any, I encourage you to create some intentions so you have purpose and believe you can impact others for good. Otherwise, you will not have a direction for where you want to go, thus you become stagnant or continually move in circles instead of moving forward. Answer the following eight questions to assist you in identifying your intentions. These are also located in your workbook:

1. Are you happy with your life? What is going well? Where do you need to make changes so you are even happier?
2. List five people you admire. What qualities, characteristics, or attributes do they possess? Do you have these traits, or do you want to develop them? Dig deep and go below the surface, do not list the superficial.
3. What are your core values, beliefs, and desires? These are your non-negotiables and deal breakers. You should be willing to end relationships or stop doing certain things so you do not go against them.
4. What is your intention for your relationship? Do you want companionship? Do you need financial support? Do you need validation? Do you believe that you are here to find a mate and grow together to create happiness and have children? Do you want a healthy relationship?

5. Do your actions align with your intentions, goals, visions, and beliefs? If they do, then the beauty of the potential relationship is that you are ready to foster deeper connections and find mutual understanding. If they do not, what do you need to change? Be honest and open with yourself.

6. List three areas you can improve in yourself. Embrace where you are but set goals to improve. Think of yourself on a ladder, you are either climbing higher or sliding lower; you cannot stay on the same rung.

7. Set your intention (how you will accomplish your goal). For example:
    Goal: I want to write a book.
    Intention: I'll write one hour every day until it is done (give yourself a deadline).

8. Choose at least one action from the following list:

    - Identify negative self-talk and write three positive thoughts you can use to replace the negative one.

    - Write down your intentions and review them daily so you are reminded of your goals.

    - Publicly declare your intention with supportive people so they can help encourage and motivate you.

    - Create a daily action plan and follow it. Break down your goal into smaller steps.

    - Determine one thing you REALLY want and focus on that. Create an action plan to accomplish it and be specific.

Take the time to answer these questions more in-depth in your workbook, then use the previous chapters such as Mindset to visualize yourself achieving these goals. Imagine what your life will look like when you accomplish these goals.

If you are like many, you may be feeling overwhelmed, unhappy, confused, or disappointed with yourself in regard to this topic. I have known many who tend to run away emotionally. You may feel like putting this book down, never to return, but do not stop now!

3. Realize Your Thoughts Lead to Action

There is a folktale about a Cherokee grandfather and his grandson that demonstrates what happens to us every day with regard to how we think and act. The grandfather was talking to his grandson about life and described how we each have an inner battle that involves two wolves. One wolf embodies evil—ego, sorrow, regret, anger, envy, arrogance, self-pity, guilt, inferiority and all that is bad. The other represents good—love, peace, joy, humility, kindness, generosity, empathy, compassion, and all that is good. The grandson then asks his grandfather which wolf wins, to which the grandfather responds, "The one you feed."[48]

When we intend to improve our lives, it is natural to have a desire to flee, fight, or even freeze. Fleeing includes running from the problems, possibly breaking up with someone, or never allowing people to get close to you for fear of being hurt. Others have a desire to fight, and they may be quickly angered, become defensive, or blame others. Others freeze, meaning they have analysis paralysis, staying in the same situation with little change. Let us explore why this happens.

Imagine walking along a hiking trail. You come around a corner and see you are twenty feet away from a mother cougar, with her babies who are about fifty feet away. She growls, and you realize she is protecting her cubs, but you instantly freeze. Fortunately, your brain does not. Instead, according to Bezdek and Telzar, your brain's hypothalamus immediately sends a signal to your pituitary gland, which then sends hormones to your adrenal gland, releasing cortisol to handle the situational stress.[49] This process is known as the hypothalamic-pituitary-adrenal (HPA) axis.

In the meantime, the amygdala makes you feel terrified and sends a signal to the HPA to react. To not get overly scared and reduce your stress, the prefrontal cortex part of your brain attempts to calm you down so you can think more clearly.

Our brain is constantly protecting us and ensuring that we do not get hurt, so it feeds us ideas that tell us not to push ourselves, to flee, fight, or freeze. We also hear the negative voice that creates self-doubt. This is perfectly natural, but if you find yourself listening to the bad wolf more than the good wolf, take a proactive approach to retraining your brain to focus on the positive. Whether it be using my *H.A.S.* Method as explained in Chapter 2 or something else, focus on the positive.

4. Become Your Intention

Take out a notecard or your workbook and list the qualities you want in your future spouse. When I made that notecard as a teenager, my intention was to find someone who met those qualities, because that is what I valued at the time. At fourteen, some of the qualities I wanted in my husband included being tall, handsome, nice, religious, educated, and a Spanish speaker. Many of those qualities were superficial. As I have matured, I added how he treats his family, peers, and coworkers, how he spends his free time, identified what he values, how he talks to others, what he believes, and observed if his actions were consistent with his words.

When I met Gordon, who did not speak Spanish and was not tall, I realized my list needed to change. I pondered why height and a foreign language were important enough to me that I would use these superficial qualities as a basis for marrying someone.

Review your notecard. Put a checkmark next to the qualities you possess. Do you possess the qualities you want in a spouse? Roger, someone close to me, faced depression and made choices leading to a hospitalization due to a drug overdose. Despite initial remorse and commitment to change, he re-associated with the crowd that negatively influenced him and fell back into destructive habits, deviating from his former happy self. By going against his values and morals, he engaged in self-destructive actions to cope with guilt, resulting in job loss and financial instability. Over a few years, I observed his struggles, hindered by pride, preventing him from seeking help. Like blindfolded individuals circling in a forest, Roger circled the drain of despair financially, mentally, emotionally, spiritually, and professionally. It is unlikely his notecard for his wife would include such behavior. The lesson here is to live the life and be the person you want to attract. If you want and desire those qualities in a mate, then possess those qualities in yourself. Expecting someone to possess qualities you lack is unrealistic and unfair to your future spouse.

5. Declare Your Intentions

When you declare your intentions, your negative wolf will talk with you even more to keep you safe. As you begin the journey of happiness, increasing your confidence, improving your self-esteem, and surrounding yourself with better people, you will feel inadequate; this is your bad wolf talking. Ignore your negative thoughts, focus on your intentions, and continue to push forward. Eventually, these feelings will be replaced with confidence and you will attract those you seek. By declaring your intentions, you are projecting your desires and giving it to the universe so you can attract what you desire.

It is imperative that you identify your intentions and your limits to what will stop you. If you are feeling discouraged, make today Day One of your new start. Learn from your past and move forward. Life is about learning and improving. We all fall down, but getting up, brushing ourselves off, and starting again is what matters. Do not give up on yourself or your dreams. Feed the good wolf and believe that your intentions are worthwhile and good. Take time now to make a change so you can be happy. I used to think that it was impossible to achieve happiness and success; that I was doomed to a life of difficulty. I feel so richly blessed now, and it is because I am relentless with my intentions. When I face life's storm, I literally smile and say, "Bring it on!" Because I now know my purpose and have set my intentions, I am committed to making it happen. This applies to life goals and my relationships.

ICEBERG INSIGHTS

The iceberg in this chapter is your intentions. Whether it be the goals you have in life or the intentions you have regarding the qualities in your future spouse, you need to have direction, which is your intention. By identifying and setting your intentions, you can then recognize how your intentions can become reality through your thoughts leading to actions and declaration. Just like climbing the metaphorical iceberg mountain, you need to have a purpose for life so you can live the life you want and attract the person you want to spend your life with. Knowing what qualities you want in a spouse will help you make choices that will attract the person you want to attract.

CHAPTER 7

Attain Non-Attachment, Correct Codependency

"Letting go of reactions and detaching from others' moods empowers us. Transitioning from reactors to being proactive, we take charge of our responses, elevating our self-esteem and gaining our independence."

Charisse Walker

I grew up in a family where my sisters typically had boyfriends, with one of them engaged during her junior and senior years of high school. Following a longstanding family tradition, my mom married at nineteen, my grandma at eighteen, and my great grandma at twenty-two. I continued this pattern by getting married at nineteen.

ACCORDING TO THE THEORY OF STRAUSS AND HOWE, history experiences four cycles before change occurs, known as the fourth turning.[50] Applying this to my family, disruptions tend to happen every eighty to one hundred years, marking a shift in family traditions. Picture a ladder where each generation ascends a rung approximately every twenty years. The fourth turning is crisis, which triggers change.

Examining the pattern from my great-grandma to me, it is evident that the family repeated the behavior of marrying at a young age. However, a significant shift occurred with my daughters, breaking this cycle and aligning with the theory of the fourth turning. The crisis manifested when my daughters experienced my divorce, marking a notable departure from the established family tradition, and they are not married.

In addition to my family's tradition, I also learned from my sisters the tendency to have a steady boyfriend. Speaking for myself, as you have read in my story as a young girl, I felt betrayed, isolated, and bullied by females. From high school, until I was married for the first time, I gravitated toward having a steady boyfriend because I felt more comfortable with males. If my relationship ended, it seemed a natural conclusion, and I naturally moved into a new relationship to ensure that I felt accepted and had companionship. My desire for a steady boyfriend marked the onset of my codependent behavior. Unfortunately, it was not until I was married to my second husband that I realized what codependency was and became aware of my harmful behavior. Fortunately, I broke free from this lifestyle, though regrettably, it happened much too late.

CODEPENDENCY

To ensure you do not fall prey to the fourth turning or codependent behavior, this chapter identifies patterns of behavior that lead to codependency. If you realize that you are codependent, use this book and workbook to achieve nonattachment status. Start by defining what codependency is and why we need to create a desire for healthy independence.

Codependency Defined

Codependency is a psychological pattern marked by excessive dependence on others for self-worth and emotional well-being, often involving unhealthy self-sacrifice and challenges in setting boundaries. It can impact individuals and relationships negatively, leading to sustained emotional abuse and one-sided dynamics.[51]

To attain nonattachment, the process begins by cultivating a positive mindset and clarifying your intentions, as discussed in preceding chapters. The next step is developing independence and self-reliance. This enables you to maintain individuality within a relationship by creating a balanced dynamic based on mutual support and shared growth.

Jim exemplifies the impact of codependency on personal well-being. Hindered by a noticeable mental disability, he struggled to form genuine friendships in high school. Trust issues persisted, and failed romantic pursuits often led to troubled and rebellious partners who gave him attention, but failed to reciprocate care. Despite experiencing heartbreak and infidelity, Jim struggled with self-confidence, settling for relationships he deep down knew were not right for him. His inability to assert boundaries and prioritize his desires, combined with mental health challenges, resulted in codependent patterns, trapping him in unhealthy connections.

Codependency's destructive impact is evident in Stacey's journey. Following her parents' split at age nine, her father's blame on her mom and subsequent disappearance left her feeling abandoned. In high school, she sought refuge in a relationship that swiftly turned abusive, with threats and coercion lasting the school year. Although she eventually broke free, her emotional wounds endured. This led to a pattern of unhealthy relationships, driven by a fear of being alone. Despite her mother's warnings about codependency, Stacy dismissed them. In her mid-twenties, she realized she needed help, but continued to grapple with breaking free from the desire to constantly have someone to be with.

Kari's story is another illustration of the detrimental impact of codependency. After high school, her sense of loneliness led her to associate with drug users who provided acceptance. Initially refraining from drug use, she eventually succumbed to peer pressure, leading to experimentation. Entering into a relationship with a troubled individual, she compromised her beliefs and values, undergoing a transformative process that altered her appearance, distanced her from her family, and involved cohabitation fueled by a deep-seated need for companionship. In the relationship, Kari assumed a caretaker role, providing unwavering support and taking on all responsibilities.

Countless stories like those of Jim, Stacey, and Kari demonstrate the profound impact of codependency, making it incredibly challenging for individuals to remove themselves from relationships they recognize are unhealthy. Many prefer enduring a dysfunctional relationship rather than facing the prospect of being alone, ultimately leading to situations that may turn abusive. Tragically, a deeper exploration often reveals a cycle of codependent behavior passed down through generations, as these individuals each came from homes where their parents, and even grandparents, exhibited similar patterns.

Identify Codependent Behavior

The good news is that the cycle can be stopped if you are willing to put in the effort and time needed to learn and correct this behavior. Codependency is a term that psychologists used first with alcoholic partners. In Sarah Kristenson's article, "15 Codependent Personality Traits and Characteristics," she discusses how codependency has become more widespread among people and gives fifteen traits to identify if you have codependent behavior.[52] I have included thirty questions in your workbook to answer to discover if you are codependent. Answer the questions in the workbook now, and then come back to this chapter.

After reading through these questions, how many did you answer yes to? Was it more than five? Ten? More? If you answered "yes" to more than ten, you may struggle with codependency. For this reason, you most likely experience some of these characteristics: ineffective communication, obsession, control issues, lack of trust, dependency, low self-esteem, boundary issues, anger, denial, repression, people pleaser, caregiver to someone because of the need to be with and help someone.

If you have a partner, or even an ex, reattempt the quiz, but this time rephrase the questions by starting with, "Does your partner...?" If you find that your partner resonates with most of these questions, reflect on whether your partner has codependent tendencies, exhibits narcissistic traits, leads you to believe you can change or "fix" them, or contributes to a potentially abusive or toxic relationship. You may be with someone because you feel obligated to assist or "fix."

If your partner engages in these behaviors, recognize you may experience sadness or entrapment when you realize you cannot alter or rescue your partner. If you find yourself feeling stuck in this situation or unsure of how to remove yourself from the relationship, acknowledge that you need significant personal growth for you to become a healthy partner who is ready to be in a relationship.

Effects of Codependent Behavior

If you answered affirmative to several of these codependent characteristics, you are more likely to end up in a toxic relationship. This will result in negative psychological outcomes that include the following emotions or actions:

+ higher levels of anxiety

+ depression, sadness

+ stress

+ resentment

+ anger

+ emotional exhaustion

+ low self-esteem

+ difficulty forming and maintaining healthy relationships

- inability to be assertive
- diminished sense of self
- reduced life satisfaction

This occurs due to a constant need to focus on meeting others' needs at the expense of your own. To counteract these tendencies, do the following:

- promote self-care
- establish healthy boundaries
- foster autonomy
- increase self-worth

For your well-being and quality of life, identifying codependency tendencies is imperative. Seeking professional help from therapists, counselors, clergy, doctors, or support groups specialized in codependency can offer personalized guidance and support to break free from codependent patterns and cultivate healthier relationships.

Causes of Codependency

Now that we understand what happens to us if we are codependent, we now need to understand what causes this behavior. Besides it being a learned and generational pattern of behavior, it is also caused by trauma. Trauma includes emotional, sexual, or physical abuse; parents who were addicted to drugs or alcohol, physical ailments, or mental disorders; parents who were overprotective or controlling; or neglect and abandonment by parents or loved ones. If we experience any of these traumas early in life, we develop a need to be loved because we did not feel loved or accepted as a child, so we latch on to someone who we think can help us feel needed. This is Maslow's third level in his hierarchy of needs.

Peggy Ferguson identifies five roles people take on in their family due to abusive or addictive family members. Table 1 explains the roles in family, the actions this role does, the feelings this role experiences, and the behavioral traits that result.[53]

Table 1: Family Roles

Title	Role in the Family	Actions in the Family	Feelings the Develop	Behavior that Results
Chief Enabler	Spouse/ Partner	Does everything to ensure the household keeps running. Compensates for partner's lack of contribution	Tries to do it all and becomes angry, fearful, guilty, resentful, or powerless as a result	Self-pity, serious (little play), self-blames, manipulates, increases responsibility, victim, martyr
Hero	Oldest Child	Becomes the star athlete or academic to reduce family pain. Attempts to improve the situation and create self-worth to the family	Tries to get a job to support the family, seeks approval and validation, is a hard worker, tries to show competence and confidence, becomes a mini-adult too soon	Inadequacy, confusion, anger, yearns for approval, appears overly confident or conceited (to hide inadequacy and fear), perfectionist, the peacemaker
Scapegoat	"Problem Child"	Becomes the distraction to the true problem	Creates problems to shift the focus from the real problem. Feels lonely, angry, fearful, hurt, rejected	Withdraws from the family and seeks out peers, acts out, defiant, depressed, rebellious, defensive, denies, disappoints, uses drugs or alcohol, has unplanned pregnancy, gets into trouble
Lost Child	Middle Child	Provides relief by becoming the forgotten child that no one worries about or focuses on	Withdraws into self, fantasizes, day dreams, will not overachieve or stand out, has few friends. Tries to hide to avoid being the problem	Lonely, hurt, inadequate, angry, quiet, aloof, withdrawn, very independent, distanced, rejects others, or quickly attaches to overcome feeling forgotten, desires companionship
Mascot	Youngest Child	Is not taken seriously, provides the comic relief	Becomes cute, funny, charming, fun. Provides laughs or happiness to release tension. The last to know the truth	Class clown to hide fear, insecurity, confusion, and loneliness. Attention seeker (appear fragile or funny), comedian

When you look at this table, do you see yourself in any of these roles? By understanding the effects of childhood trauma, you can then identify how you became codependent. For example, if you were the Mascot, you are likely to marry the Hero or Enabler to create more consistency, and security, but your mate could be more abusive and controlling. The Hero might choose a Scapegoat because the Hero wants to fix or help. If your mate is an addict, the Hero might then become the Enabler so you have more control. Lastly, if you were a Lost Child, you might latch on to someone quickly, or push people away because you are comfortable by yourself and do not trust people. There are so many scenarios, so take time to evaluate your current and past relationships to see if you or your partner are stuck in one of these roles.

Fixing Codependency

Once you identify your role, to change your behavior you need to accept that it is a problem, and be willing to make a change. When addressing codependent tendencies, it is essential to establish personal space and cultivate independence within your relationship. By doing so, you enhance your sense of security and confidence in yourself. This process fosters autonomy, allowing you to develop your unique identity and individuality.

In the initial stages of a relationship, the thrill of newfound love often sparks enthusiasm and a desire for connection, leading to a willingness to accommodate your partner's preferences to spend more time together. While prioritize each other is normal initially, over time, both partners need to express interest in each other's activities and allow space for your own pursuits. This aspect is further explored in Chapter 15.

While dating, it is fun to explore your partner's interests, but it is essential to preserve your individual interests, hobbies, goals, and values that define you as an individual. This practice not only allows you to pursue your passions and engage in activities that bring you joy, but also safeguards against feeling suffocated or developing codependency. Creating alone time, ensuring privacy, and making personal decisions are key to maintaining your individuality. Whether it is finding a new hobby, pursuing a passion, watching a movie, taking a class solo, or simply going for a walk alone, these activities contribute to your sense of self.

When you notice you are losing yourself to please your mate, alter your behavior for fear of his reaction, or find your mate getting upset because you are not doing what he wants you to do, heed the following three C's as taken from Homestead Schools:[54]

+ Cause: You are not the cause of your mate's problems or anger.

+ Control: Your mate chooses his feelings and actions, you cannot control or change

+ Cure: No matter how much you want to, you are not the cure to his problems.

If you find your mate getting upset and blaming you for his anger, remember these three Cs.

The Importance of Time Together

Have you heard the phrase "absence makes the heart grow fonder?" In many instances, being away from each other to pursue separate interests and create new experiences allows an opportunity to share new stories and bring new perspectives into the relationship. This helps prevent the relationship from becoming stagnant. By respecting each other's personal space, more trust grows in your partner's decision-making capability, judgment, and ability to handle personal matters. Be cautious though, I have watched far too many couples break up because they either felt suffocated, became apathetic to the relationship, or grew apart. Apathy opens the door to your mate finding someone who does care, do not grow distant.

Some people wonder how much time is healthy to spend together. The answer varies for each couple. Some couples do everything together, while other couples spend most of their time apart, even sleeping on different levels in the same house. Think of a zero to ten scale. On one end it says, "None of Your Time" (0) while the other end says, "All of Your Time" (10). When you are in a relationship, what number on the scale do you find yourself wanting to spend time with your mate? What number on the scale does your mate say? Do not compare yourself to any other couple and how they spend their time together; figure out what works for you and communicate with each other. This allows you to create a balance between togetherness and independence, which is critical to a healthy relationship.

Sometimes we tend to control each other's time. If you find yourself doing this, identify your motivation. Is it because you feel insecure and do not realize you are doing it? If your partner does it to you, identify her motivation. Open and honest conversations about your needs, wants, and expectations are critical to creating a healthy relationship. If you do not feel you can approach your mate, or believe your concerns will fall on deaf ears, this is a red flag. Talk with a trusted advisor about how to proceed in your relationship, or decide if you even should. I cannot stress the detrimental effects codependency has on people. I have personally lived it and seen its effects. Creating nonattachment is an important skill to develop while still desiring companionship.

ICEBERG INSIGHTS

Codependency is an obstacle that many people struggle with. Much like a submerged mass of an iceberg, the true depth of codependency is often hidden beneath the surface, affecting personal relationships and emotional well-being. Codependency, characterized by an excessive reliance on others for validation and a sense of self-worth, becomes a formidable obstacle to personal growth and autonomy. It hinders your ability to navigate life independently, stifling individuality and fostering a reliance on external factors for emotional stability. By addressing and understanding the implications of codependency, this chapter aims to empower you to break free from these emotional shackles so you can chart a course toward self-discovery, ultimately leading to healthier, more fulfilling relationships.

CHAPTER 8

Give Yourself Grace

"Embracing growth feels uneasy as it introduces a version of yourself you haven't encountered. Be kind to yourself, take a breath, and navigate through it with grace."

CHARISSE WALKER

While being nailed to a cross after enduring hours of torture and pain, Jesus Christ loved those who treated him unkindly so much so that he said, "Father, forgive them; for they know not what they do."[55] This was the ultimate act of forgiveness, love, and kindness. For someone perfect, he experienced betrayal, abandonment, loss, and horrific treatment by those he loved.

REMEMBER THE STORY OF THE GOOD AND BAD wolves in Chapter 6? As you continue to progress on your journey to heal yourself, the bad wolf will tell you that you are failing, that you do not deserve happiness, and that what you want is unattainable. By dying on the cross, Jesus made it possible for us to attain forgiveness and peace. To this end, it is possible to find peace, healing, and happiness, through grace.

We all know it is easier said than done as the bad wolf whispers negativity in our ear. This happened to Martin Luther King, Jr. while reflecting at his kitchen table, feeling the weight of recent threats—menacing calls, ominous letters, and death threats. Fear for his wife, newborn daughter, and himself lingered as he navigated the personal consequences of his commitment to the civil rights movement. He prayed to God and expressed how he was losing his courage. While praying, King said he heard an inner voice, who he believed was Jesus, telling him to "Stand up for righteousness. Stand up for justice. Stand up for truth. And lo, I will be with you. Even until the end of the world."[56] Almost instantly, King's uncertainty disappeared.

GRACE, ACT, COURAGE

We may not directly hear Jesus's voice, but rest assured, He is with us and can guide us through any challenge if we open ourselves to Him. In a talk given at Brigham Young University, Jonathan G. Sandberg explained that healing requires courage, action, and grace.[57] Although this is true, I believe that for true healing, these attributes should be reordered as grace, action, and courage. Let us explore each trait further.

Grace

We start with grace because when you make mistakes, it is easy to get upset and discouraged with yourself. You may doubt yourself, and feel like you will never be able to change, that it is not possible to be forgiven, but it is! That is the journey of healing. EcoLips suggests five ways to give yourself grace, which I have tweaked.[58]

1. Be real, not perfect.
Accepting yourself and embracing authenticity are much healthier approaches than striving for unattainable perfection. Here are two instances illustrating the detrimental effects of the pursuit of perfectionism.

In my journey, the pressure to excel in every aspect of my life dominated my mindset prior to college. Fueled by a perfectionist drive, I pushed myself to the limits, resulting in severe stomach problems I later learned were attributed to self-imposed stress. Diagnosed with severe chronic fatigue during my freshman year of college, doctors suggested I drop out until I recovered. However, my determination to graduate in four years took precedence over my healing. Choosing to stay in school required a significant shift from my relentless pursuit of perfection to a more realistic approach.

Embracing the concept of granting myself grace, I accepted that if I could honestly look at myself in the mirror and confidently say I gave my best effort, then I could not expect anything further. This shift towards realism and self-compassion became a crucial aspect of my personal growth and acceptance.

Another example happened in a neighborhood I once called home. There, I witnessed a stark contrast among women. While many were kind, generous, and talented, others projected an image of perfection and engaged in fierce competition. This environment took a toll, turning some into bullies, while others experienced isolation. A few individuals went further, rebelling against the prevailing religious culture, choosing to distance themselves entirely.

This contrast highlights the importance of embracing realism and grace while rejecting the harmful effects of perfectionism for a healthier and more authentic community.

2. Mistakes are normal.

As humans, we are prone to making mistakes. The crucial aspect lies in the lessons we learn from these errors. Rather than indulging in self-pity or embarrassment, it is essential to embrace your mistakes with humility, study them, and move forward. Dwelling on the past only anchors you in the past; instead, focus on growth and progression. Here is one example of embracing our choices.

Soon after Jody graduated high school she became pregnant. She gave her daughter, Libby, up for adoption and eventually married and had her own family. When each of her children turned twelve, she sat them down and explained that they had a sibling. Jody explained the situation and encouraged them to be careful and to choose their actions wisely. Because she was honest, her children trusted her and they all married before having children. Now that Libby's adoptive parents passed away, Jody reconnected with her. Jody could have felt guilty for giving up Libby, but for decades, Jody's marriage was tumultuous. Had Jody kept Libby, she would have grown up in a very tumultuous environment. Instead, Libby grew up in a secure, happy, and healthy home. Sometimes "mistakes" are not mistakes, so allow yourself grace.

3. Say no to things. You do not have to do everything.
I grew up in a very service-oriented and religious family. I love both, but I realized that had I not learned to say no during my college days, I would most likely be stressed, depressed, overcommitted, and unhappy because I would be living my life to please others. It is OK to say no. You do not have to volunteer for, or do, everything.

Zoe learned this important lesson while sitting in a mastermind. She revealed she had been trying to have a baby. She and her husband had been through numerous rounds of in vitro fertilization (IVF) and suffered multiple miscarriages. She stated she was torn because she wanted to do all the activities that our coach was suggesting, but worried that if she did, the stress would prevent her from conceiving. I told her that it was okay to say no. In our lives, there are different seasons to accomplish our goals. For me, raising kids and not being able to be a full-time, stay-at-home mom was devastating. When I finally had the opportunity to be a mom, I took it! I explained to her that she needed to enjoy the season she was in, which was to be a mom, and to stop worrying about giving 100 percent of herself to the industry she was at the mastermind for. She now has a baby because she gave herself grace and learned to say no, which reduced her stress, and allowed her to focus on what was most important to her.

4. Enjoy "me time."
Many of us are taught to be charitable and serve others. If we refrain from giving we are often labeled as selfish or feel a sense of guilt for not helping. Striking a balance between acts of charity and personal time is a delicate task. It is essential to allocate time for "me time" to maintain your mental well-being. It does not have to take a lot of time; thirty minutes to an hour is sufficient. Whether it be exercising, enjoying a massage, watching a movie, getting a pedicure, going for a walk, or taking a drive, do something to replenish your well-being. Schedule me time and prioritize it!

As a mom and wife, it is hard to not feel guilty about taking me time. I used to feel selfish because that was an hour or two that I could have been helping my children, cooking, cleaning, or teaching. However, imagine a bucket full of water. Every time you do something for someone, you take a cup of water out of the bucket and fill someone else's bucket. Whether single or married, if you keep taking from your bucket and giving to others and never filling your own, eventually you will run out and have nothing else to give. Since I have many more years left to rear children, I realized the importance of taking time to replenish my own bucket by doing things for myself.

5. Find positivity every day and be proud of one thing you have done.
It is easy to become negative and feel like you are not progressing. Before ending your day, identify at least one activity you are proud of for the day and three things you are grateful for, be specific. Celebrate your wins. By focusing on the good you have done, you will develop more confidence, increase your health, and feel successful.

Learning to heal requires having grace with yourself.

Act

When you experience trauma, it is tempting to dwell on it, letting it shape your identity and becoming a victim. This may lead to feeling angry towards God for allowing such adversity. Instead of extending grace to yourself and embracing healing, you risk allowing life to pass you by, becoming a passive observer of your existence.

While you may recognize the need for change and express the desire to do so, true transformation requires more than words. It demands planning, taking action, and implementing that plan. Regaining control of your life shifts your perspective. Rather than remaining a victim, you can alter your outlook, viewing the trials you endure as a path to strength and a means to positively impact others.

Choosing positivity is not a passive decision; it requires intentional action. Whether it is in the pursuit of financial success, self-improvement, or healing, active participation is fundamental. Healing necessitates taking an active role in the process. Dwelling on past traumas without overcoming them leads to stagnation; true healing occurs when you actively engage in the process and move beyond the impact of the trauma.

Courage

The final component of the healing formula is courage. After my senior year, I was invited to a banquet for a scholarship I won for the California/Nevada region. When I arrived, they took me to a platform where I would sit above the crowd, read my essay, and then receive my award. Imagine eating lunch in front of everyone and then address the large crowd. How many times have you felt anxious about being in the spotlight, eating in front of others, or public speaking?

Confronting all three challenges at seventeen years old was overwhelming for me. The fear of spilling my lunch in my lap, having food stuck in my teeth, or accidentally propelling food onto someone after I cut it haunted my thoughts. Despite these worries, my commitment remained steadfast during the five-hour drive to the event. Upon arrival, they directed me onto the platform to speak. As the food was served,

I initially stared at it with fear. However, looking out at the large crowd, I realized no one was focused on me; they were engrossed in their own conversations and meals. With that realization, I took a bite, then another, and finished my food without incident. When it came time to read my essay, I did it smoothly and collected my award without a hitch.

Think of a time when you were terrified or anxious about an event or someone's reaction. If you cannot think of one, consider moments like dancing, speaking, competing in a sport, first day of school or work, or a date. We often build up such scenarios in our minds that it becomes hard to breathe or think. Yet, if we are courageous and face our fears, the event usually unfolds smoothly. If not, at least it is over.

Sandberg provides three additional steps to develop courage to change:

1. Face the truth about what needs to change.
John 8:32 states, "Ye shall know the truth, and the truth shall make you free."[59] Be honest with yourself, even if you do not want to be. I had a friend who had no idea of the self-destructive behavior he was inflicting upon himself and others. He denied his actions until he was shown the truth. Once he realized the full scope of his behavior, he accepted the gravity of the problem, allowing him to begin the journey to healing and self-improvement.

2. Be congruent in your behavior.
Consistency in behavior across various situations is crucial. Consider the scenario where a friend consistently criticizes her partner in private but publicly expresses love and appreciation on social media. Such inconsistency erodes trust and integrity. Personally, witnessing such behavior leads me to question her sincerity, as there appears to be a lack of alignment between her words and actions. Cultivating

the courage to be consistently honest and sincere, guided by your moral compass, is challenging but essential for building trust and maintaining integrity.

3. Stand up for your beliefs.

We all have different beliefs about how to behave and what is right or wrong. Thomas S. Monson stated, "Let us have the courage to defy the consensus, the courage to stand for principle. Courage, not compromise . . . A moral coward is afraid to do what he thinks is right because others will disapprove or laugh."[60]

Having the courage to stand up for what you believe is right is scary but necessary. If your actions deviate from what you know is right, quickly correct your behavior and return to the right path. When faced with a situation that contradicts your beliefs and you lack the courage to speak up, then leave. Upholding integrity and staying true to your convictions is not only beneficial to yourself, but also to those around you. In some instances, people are looking for a leader to be the example so they can follow suit. Be that leader.

It may be tempting to join the bandwagon and contribute to the negativity in a situation, but succumbing to such behavior has detrimental effects on you and your relationship. Granting yourself grace, taking actions that aligns with your beliefs, even when it is challenging, provides the courage needed to persist on the path toward self-improvement.

ICEBERG INSIGHTS

In this chapter, the metaphorical iceberg represents the journey of self-discovery and healing through grace. Grace involves taking intentional actions despite internal hesitations, and summoning the courage to confront self-doubt and fears, thereby initiating the healing process. Submerged beneath the surface are obstacles resembling past traumas and unresolved emotional wounds that demand acknowledgment and careful navigation. To stay true to yourself, you need to establish boundaries and confront external pressures, both societal and peer-related. Additionally, the challenges of lacking support and engaging in negative self-talk emerge as formidable icebergs. Recognizing and addressing these hidden complexities sets you on a path of self-discovery, resilience, and empowerment. Ultimately, navigating these obstacles leads to the grace that accompanies authenticity and personal growth.

PART II

Think back to your first boyfriend or girlfriend. Do you recall envisioning a future where you would marry her? I vividly remember signing my name with his last name, as if it was a foregone conclusion. Often, our initial crushes or puppy love make us believe we have found our soulmate, even though we hardly know the person. In relationships, especially during the early stages, the intensity of infatuation causes us to overlook red flags. However, identify these warning signs prior to fully committing to a relationship.

WHEN I ENTERED THE DATING SCENE AFTER MY DIVORCE, I applied the principles outlined in Part II to assess potential partners. If I sensed that someone was not a suitable long-term companion, I ended the courtship.

Now that you have completed Part I, you have prepared yourself to enter a relationship by **Finding** the iceberg, overcome **Limiting** beliefs, listened to your **Intuition**, broken free from external **Pressures**, embraced your **Potential**, acted with **Intention**, cultivated **Non-Attachment**, and granted yourself **Grace**. Notice, these bold words create the acronym, "F.L.I.P.P.I.N.G."

Welcome to the second part of this book where we envision your potential mate as an iceberg, with most his personality concealed beneath the surface, beyond casual observation. Just as ship captains navigate waters while avoiding hidden dangers, exploring a romantic relationship involves uncovering the depths of your partner's personality. I term this process "flipping the iceberg," encouraging you to look beyond surface impressions.

Throughout this section, we explore essential aspects of this endeavor, from seeing beyond first **Impressions** to understanding **Commitment**, arming yourself with tools for relationship nurturing, **Educating** yourself on handling situations and personalities, identifying emotional **Baggage**, understanding the pivotal role of setting **Expectations**, and **Recognizing** subtle nuances of abuse within relationships, and finally emphasizing the indispensable principle of balance—the art of both **Giving and Receiving**. This section uses the acronym, **I.C.E.B.E.R.G.** to equip you with skills to flip your partner's iceberg so you can uncover his hidden self and find the truths that originally lay beneath his iceberg. Once you identify his true self, you can make an informed decision about whether or not he will be your spouse, and you can create a lasting marriage.

CHAPTER 9

Look Beyond the First Impressions / Façade

"First impressions are the doorway to potential connections; with time, research, and intuition, we navigate beyond, revealing whether they lead to meaningful relationships or closed opportunities."

CHARISSE WALKER

Think of the last conversation you had with someone you have not seen for at least two weeks. Did the conversation follow this familiar pattern?

> Bob: Hi! How are you?
> You: Good, and you?
> Bob: Good!

But are you both genuinely good? It is highly unlikely. So, why has this become the standard greeting, and what purpose does it serve? Why not just exchange cheek kisses or hugs and say, "Hi! I've missed you!

Imagine the conversation like this instead:

Bob: Hi! How are you?

You: Not good! I am so stressed, I haven't been getting much sleep, my house is a mess, my child is struggling in school, work is hectic, I feel fat, and I have been struggling with the worst pain I have experienced in a while. I feel like my kids are raising themselves and I just want to lay in bed and sleep all day. How about you?

OFTEN, WE EXCHANGE THESE "I'M GOOD" PLEASANTRIES out of habit or as a conversation filler. We are typically in a rush and do not have time for an in-depth answer. Consequently, we have learned to make a good first impression, especially with acquaintances. Have you ever answered honestly, taking the time to do so? How did you or the other person react? I tested this approach at the doctor's office. When the medical assistant asked how I was, I replied, "I would love a do-over to last Thursday."

He responded with, "Oh," finished what he needed, and then left the room. The next person that came in also asked how I was. I responded the same. She then chuckled and said, "I'm sorry," and the conversation ended.

People often ask, "How are you?" not seeking an honest answer but aiming for a conversation filler, acknowledgement, or deeper connection. This is an example of our learned superficiality. We are taught to put on a facade from a young age to hide our true feelings. We strive to present our best selves to gain acceptance. Interestingly, we often prioritize the opinions of strangers over loved ones when it comes to emotional outbursts.

This behavior is akin to showing only the "tip of the iceberg." Like a king, we maintain a polite, cordial, and politically correct demeanor in public, symbolized by the crown atop his head. It is the persona we want to project, the visible part above the waterline, concealing the real person both above and below the water's surface.

Here are three examples illustrating how facades deceive us. In the first example, I recognized a former neighbor while waiting in line for popcorn at the movie theater. He and his wife had it all—looks, success, cute kids, and a beautiful home. They were the envy of many in the neighborhood. To my surprise, I saw him with another woman and her children while at the movies. I thought maybe it was his sister visiting and looked around for his wife but did not see her. As I walked up to say hi, I saw him interact with this woman in such a way that I knew it was not his sister. Unsure of how to respond, I felt relieved that we were wearing masks during the pandemic so he could not recognize me as I quickly backpedaled. I later learned this couple divorced and he was with his new wife and her children. This couple appeared to have it all, but behind the facade their marriage was rocky and crumbled.

The second example involves Billy and Jenny, a couple I once envied for their seemingly-perfect relationship. Jenny showered Billy with praise in public, leaving me envious. However, after a few years I discovered that Jenny was unhappy, and Billy was far from the perfect partner. Their facade concealed the pain they both felt personally and in their relationship.

The last story illustrates the discrepancy between external appearance and internal struggles within a relationship. Having recently escaped from an abusive marriage, Bailey sought solace in a man who, on the surface appeared ambitious, confident, talented, and outgoing, resulting in a swift marriage. Soon after marriage, the facade crumbled as Barry revealed a starkly different persona at home—angry, stubborn, neglectful of household and financial responsibilities, and lacking self-confidence, ambition, and energy. To friends, family, and acquaintances, he maintained that facade of the person Bailey thought she married, but at home, he was very different.

Bailey loved Barry deeply, but she felt she made a mistake marrying him. Unfortunately, she did not want her loved ones to know how she felt because she ignored their warnings prior to her marriage. Despite her internal sadness, Bailey portrayed a facade of happiness and solidarity regarding her decision to marry Barry. Behind closed doors she sobbed in solitude for years, highlighting the profound impact of maintaining a facade in the face of personal turmoil.

Today, putting on a facade is prevalent, especially due to social media. Research shows a significant increase in teen suicide, depression, and anxiety over the past two decades, with a 60 percent rise in depression among youth aged fourteen to seventeen from 2009 to 2017.[61] This trend is linked to the extensive use of technology, particularly social media platforms where people easily project a false image. Social media community sites are wrought with deception, portraying the fake self.

We all put on a false self at some point. Jealousy would be less common if we truly understood each person's reality. Given that we all possess flaws, insecurities, make mistakes, and face challenges, acknowledging our imperfections should be normal, but it is not. As a result, the task at hand with our partner is to discover these imperfections to assess whether they are acceptable before deciding to pursue a long-term relationship.

In the early stages of dating and falling in love, we tend to overlook flaws and red flags, focusing solely on positive qualities. This "honeymoon" phase of a relationship leads people to be on their best behavior—acting happier, healthier, more thoughtful, and caring. However, as the relationship progresses, the initial novelty fades, and the issues we initially appreciated or justified can become sources of annoyance or frustration.

Genuine love flourishes in an environment of trust and honesty. Prior to marriage, your objective is to unveil your partner's authentic self, fostering a foundation where trust and honesty can effortlessly thrive. Instances of dishonesty from your partner may point to underlying issues within the relationship or with your partner. With time, lies unravel as they give rise to inconsistencies, eventually leading to exposure. Therefore, it is crucial to pay attention and give the relationship the time needed for any dishonesty to be revealed.

A good example of unveiling the real self happened during the Covid pandemic that created an era I call "Zoomland." During this time, people shifted to remote work, leading to many online meetings via Zoom. Initially, everyone dressed professionally and presented their best self, from the waist up. As time passed, people became more comfortable with being on camera, some even forgot they were on camera and unmuted themselves during meetings, engaging in embarrassing behaviors, such as nose-picking, wearing only underwear, yelling at their children, and commenting on the facilitator. This is just one example of the honeymoon phase moving into revealing their true selves as they let their guard down.

A notable example of this was a California school board, that unknowingly conducted an open meeting where they criticized parents' concerns about remote learning. Board members were overheard by parents making disparaging and accusatory remarks about parents while using profanity, thinking the meeting was private. Parents heard the conversation and let the board members know they were listening.[62] The board members were comfortable with each other, but put on a facade with parents. This time their true selves were revealed and they resigned the next day.

Imagine if the iceberg that struck the Titanic was sticking more than halfway out of the water instead of below. The lookout may have spotted it sooner and the collision could have been avoided, or at least minimized. This may have resulted in more lives saved. Instead, despite the warning signs from other ships, they chose to push on. Warning signs abound in various situations, but the challenge lies in our tendency to disregard the warning signs or not see them at all. How can we recognize these warning signs and uncover the underlying issues sooner? By utilizing your time, intuition, and research.

Time

While there is no set timeframe for dating before marriage, a practical guideline is to date for a full year, experiencing all the seasons together to observe how your partner behaves in various settings. Success stories abound, from couples who married after two weeks and are still together fifty years later to those who dated for two years only to divorce within months. In the 1900s, committing to marriage was more common, but today's statistics reveal a higher divorce rate among baby boomers. During their original marriages, cultural norms often dictated staying together for the sake of the children, marrying the first person they were intimate with or had a baby with, or simply marrying young due to cultural norms. With changing cultural norms and grown children, many baby boomers now realize they do not have to remain in unhappy marriages. The key is to take the time needed to truly discover each other before making such a significant commitment.

Ginger and Julio's relationship exemplifies the impact of culture and time on romantic connections. When Julio and Ginger first met, Julio knew she was "The One." Julio was outgoing, talented, happy, fun, and generous. Ginger enjoyed her time with Julio. As they continued to date, Julio solidified his decision to marry Ginger, but Ginger felt they were not compatible. Trying to convince herself that Julio was right for her, the two continued to date. Two years passed and Ginger felt like she had spent so much time with him that she needed to make it work. Eventually she realized that no amount of time would change how she felt and they ended the relationship.

Just because your partner may think you are the one, it does not mean you will feel the same. Take the time you need to get to know your partner so you can make your own decision. If you know he is not right for you, do not prolong the inevitable. It is not fair to your partner and precious time is wasted for both of you.

Intuition

During our first few months of dating, George showered me with affection and gifts, making me feel like a queen. Anything I needed he was there for me. He spoiled me rotten and even thought of things I needed before I did to help me and my family. He taught me how I deserved to be treated by a partner and I thought there was potential with him. Sometimes our hearts trick our minds and gut. Often, narcissists, abusers, and manipulators may initially shower you with gifts, but these gifts come with a price that result in anger and control if they do not get their way. It is essential to trust your intuition and to have faith and the courage to listen to your instincts and loved ones to avoid bad relationships. We discussed intuition in detail in Chapter 3, so revisit that chapter to understand more about the importance of your intuition.

Research

When your partner tells you something, listen. Follow up on what she tells you by validating, clarifying, and researching. Take time to ask each other the questions in your *Flipping the Iceberg Workbook* and other conversations. After you have been dating for a while or in an exclusive relationship and he says he does not look at pornography, check his phone. If she says she is not dating or flirting with anyone else, check her phone. Although you should be able to trust each other, during this phase there should not be secrets between you. Please understand, there is a fine line between being intrusive or controlling and validation, so be aware and respectful.

If your judgment is clouded, then rely on the perspective of family, friends, coworkers, children, and even pets. Loved ones often have an intuitive sense about our relationships. Consider instances where you or a loved one said, "I don't think that person is right for you," only for them, or you, to ignore the comment, and then hear, "I told you so" later. People with experience or without emotional bias provide valuable insights, so remain open-minded, question their opinions, and assess feedback, removing your bias as much as possible.

Pets possess an innate sense and are not easily deceived by the false self. When you leave the room, your partner might act differently towards your pet, revealing aspects of her true behavior that you may not witness. Your pet can serve as a valuable resource when evaluating your potential partner.

Being more aware of your support systems' comments and openly listening to their opinions allows you to see, or even trust that there is an iceberg ahead, ultimately preventing you from sinking. Luckily, I heeded my sister's insight, preventing me from making a serious mistake with George, from the intuition section. One day he picked me up for a date. I walked outside and he ran inside to use the bathroom. A few minutes later, he walked out, and my sister followed him out, yelling at him.

I got out of the car and asked her what was wrong, she turned to me and warned me about him. She told me, in front of him, that he was a liar, controlling, and a manipulator. She then repeated some things he said to her, which he denied as she said it. He had always been nice to me, and I thought she was acting crazy, so I dismissed her. As we headed back to the car, she yelled to me to start watching for certain behaviors and I will thank her later.

We continued to date, and sure enough, over time, subtle warning signs emerged until they were blatant and he became controlling, jealous, and prone to temper tantrums. I realized there was no future with him, prompting me to end the relationship. Unfortunately, initial generosity came with expectations, and he used manipulation tactics when I distanced myself from him. Had I listened to my intuition I would have avoided the relationship, but fortunately with time and research I saw the truth and ended the relationship prior to marriage.

ICEBERG INSIGHT

The facade is the 10 percent you see above the water. The other 90 percent below the water looks much different, so flip the iceberg to uncover the truth. Look beyond the façade. Sooner or later his true self will be revealed if you give the relationship time, research what you are told, and use your intuition. Rushing to judgement based solely on surface impressions is unwise. Dig deeper by questioning, verifying, observing, and continually exploring. Your goal is to identify the potential iceberg ahead, ultimately preventing you and the relationship from sinking.

CHAPTER 10

Make the Commitment

**"A strong commitment intertwines two lives,
enduring even through challenging times."**

CHARISSE WALKER

As a child, I believed my purpose was to get married, have kids, stay home, and take care of them and our home. Maybe watching numerous classic movies set in the 1950s and 60s with all the perfect houses placed side by side in sweet suburbia, watching the perfect, happy family gave me that idea. I graduated high school at seventeen and started college at the same age. By the time I was engaged, I had almost two years of living on my own under my belt and thought I was ready for marriage. Boy was I naive!

TO ME, COMMITMENT MEANT FINISHING COLLEGE in four years and staying true to my faith. Since every boyfriend I had before my first husband ended in a breakup, I did not understand the magnitude of the decision I was making. Marriage means staying true to your commitment "til death do you part," or for eternity. It also signifies that you are willing to invest time, focus, and effort into nurturing the relationship and making it a priority. Commitment plays a crucial role in the success and longevity of a relationship because it helps build the foundation for stability, trust, and security. By committing, you agree to be dedicated and loyal to each other and the partnership forever. I figured I was in love and love would conquer all. It never occurred to me that if I had any doubts, I should hold off until I was sure.

To see how others viewed commitment while teaching a class on relationships, I surveyed numerous couples in both successful and unsuccessful relationships and asked them what the secret to a healthy marriage was. I received all sorts of suggestions that included going to bed at the same time, never going to bed angry, talking things through, having patience and tolerance, maintaining your hobbies, overlooking all faults and seeing them as God does, but one suggestion from Cheryl stuck out to me. She said, you must be willing to let the person act their role, and then that person must be willing to accept the responsibilities for the decisions they make.

For example, Marty was the breadwinner and wanted to quit his job. Shannon was the stay-at-home wife and mom, and her role was to manage the family and household. If Marty quit, he knew he was responsible for supporting the family. This was the agreement they made prior to their marriage. If either person wanted to switch roles or alter the agreement, they needed to communicate their desire and agree. Allowing your partner to follow through on his commitment is hard, but that is how you grow closer, build trust, and build confidence with each other and yourself.

Marriage means that you are covenanting and making vows that demonstrate your love and devotion to your partner and God. By committing to marriage, you are saying that you promise to do certain things, no matter what. This means that you are committed through thick and thin and will not back out when it gets hard or if you disagree. I highly recommend that you have no doubts coming from your intuition, faith, family, or friends when you enter this covenant and that you are at peace with yourself and your relationship. It is natural to be nervous, but that is different from feeling it is not the right decision.

ARE YOU READY FOR MARRIAGE

Marriage.com identified fifteen signs to look for to see if you and your potential spouse are ready for marriage.[63] I have altered and expanded on this list to help you identify potential red flags that also need to be addressed before marriage. As you read through this list, use your workbook to delve deeper into the questions. Be honest with yourself in your responses.

1. You have only known your soon-to-be spouse for a short while.
Chapter 9 discusses dating four seasons so that you see your mate in as many situations as possible. The time you have together needs to be quality time. Talk, ask, get to know each other, research how they are, and verify by watching what they do.

2. You are uncomfortable sharing your secrets.
Yes, the deep, dark ones. If your future spouse cannot trust you to share his secrets, then what else will he not trust you with? Do you feel comfortable sharing your deepest secrets? This is potentially a huge problem as seen by the examples below.

> A. Thomas and Roxy have been married for over ten years and have kids together. One day a child shows up claiming she is Thomas's daughter. Roxy thought she was Thomas's first intimate partner. Thomas knew about his daughter, but was afraid to tell his wife.

> B. Greg and Suzanne marry after dating for a year. They never fought and were devoted to each other. A month into their marriage, Suzanne found out Greg had been flirting with multiple girls online, even after they married.

These couples do not trust each other. Think about what you are withholding from your future spouse. Let me clarify, you do not need to share everything with your partner, but if your partner asks you point blank, do not lie! Use your workbook to answer more questions on this topic. If you are fearful of being judged or rejected by your partner, then you are not ready to be in a long-term relationship with that person. I do not recommend you be an open book from the first date, but as the relationship progresses and you still do not feel you can be honest or feel your mate is holding something back, this is a red flag.

3. You have never had a fight.

You will undoubtedly have diverse approaches to conflict from your mate, ranging from avoiding it, to explosive outbursts, to the silent treatment, to refusing to budge. Successful couples, however, navigate disagreements through productive discussions that lead to win/win resolutions and a deeper understanding of each other's perspectives. If fights lack resolution or productivity, it may indicate unreadiness for marriage. The ability to address and resolve issues before marriage is crucial; you must be willing to discuss your feelings openly and find compromises. Learning effective communication during disagreements before marriage lays the foundation for navigating challenges as a united front. By proactively addressing conflicts and being willing to rock the boat and discuss concerns, you enhance your chances of building a strong, lasting relationship that can weather the inevitable storms of married life.

4. You are just as entitled to your opinion as your mate.

We all have opinions about issues. Whether we agree or disagree, both opinions matter. You owe it to yourself and your mate to discuss the hard topics before marriage so you can decide if the opposing viewpoints are deal breakers or not. Waiting until after you are married to discuss the big issues and be honest about your opinion is too late. Your spouse might question why you hid your opinion from him and wonder what else you have hidden under the surface. In addition, if your partner consistently disregards your opinions, that is also a red flag.

5. Your values do not align.

When values do not align in a relationship, it can be very difficult to work through and are often deal breakers. It is easier when it is just the two of you, but when you have children, which values will your children follow? Topics to discuss include religion, how money is spent, how you spend your time, and what is important to each of you. Avoid major conflicts in the future by discussing your values now. These topics are discussed further in Chapter 13 of this book.

6. You have a wandering eye; have secret, intimate conversations with your ex; or continue to flirt with your office workers, customers, or others.

Is the attention of your mate not enough for you? If not, why do you need additional validation from others besides your mate? It is okay to talk to others or appreciate the characteristics of others, but you should be completely satisfied, happy, and seek validation from your mate, not others.

7. You wonder if you are ready to settle down.

You may enjoy your mate but wonder if you should continue dating. After my divorce, I was not looking to jump back into a marriage. Nine months after my divorce was final, I met Gordon. Although our relationship progressed quickly, I was not ready to settle down. My intuition told me to date others, so I followed my feelings. Although he was single for a long time and was ready to marry me, he gave me the space I needed. By dating others, I realized he was who I wanted to be with. Because I did not rush into a marriage, I felt more secure about my decision. Do not feel pressured into settling down, but also be aware of your fears. Are you sabotaging a good relationship and missing out when you may actually be ready?

8. You do not like to compromise.

When you are younger, flexibility and adaptability in your habits are more common because you are not yet set in your ways as you are still discovering your likes and dislikes. Conversely, with age comes ingrained habits and resistance to altering established ways, making it a challenge to embrace change for a new partner. The essence of compromise, explored in Chapter 15, becomes crucial in relationships. Take, for instance, differing weekend routines—you may want to sleep in while your mate enjoys getting up early, getting chores done and enjoying the rest of the day.

Your willingness to compromise determines your success in your relationship. If you are compelled to give up habits without genuine readiness, resentment may follow. True commitment to a relationship surfaces when love surpasses your attachment to personal habits, fostering an environment for mutual growth. Evaluating whether you and your partner is willing to adjust habits for each other's happiness is integral to sustaining a healthy relationship, where genuine introspection and honesty play important roles.

9. You feel pressured to settle down, especially if your friends have married or have kids.

The prospect of lifelong companionship brings joy and excitement, making dating an enjoyable journey of getting to know each other. However, the perception of finding "The One" may not always be mutual. Marriage, a sacred commitment involving you, your spouse, and God demands careful consideration. Resist societal pressure or familial expectations; the decision to marry should be deeply personal. If friends or family exert undue influence, prioritize your own readiness over external expectations. Establish clear boundaries and communicate your stance, emphasizing the importance of making the right decision rather than succumbing to societal pressures. Also, just because the person you are dating feels you are her soulmate does not mean you feel the same way, do not feel pressured to settle just because your partner feels it is right. Chapter 4 further explores this topic.

10. You think your spouse will change.

I hear this so often: "She has potential, she can change." Change in a person only happens if she desires it. While we all have the potential for change, the key factor is the individual's motivation to change. If you believe you can change your potential spouse, reconsider, as true transformation is a personal choice made by the individual.

I had a conversation with someone whose wife divorced him. He said, "It's my fault. I married her young enough, I should've trained her to be what I wanted." You should not need to change anyone. You should be happy with who they are, not hope to train them to be who you want.

Motivation for change can be classified into two categories: extrinsic (external) and intrinsic (internal). Extrinsic motivation, often fueled by external pressures or requests, tends to be short-lived, leading to temporary change, resentment, or no change at all. For lasting transformation, individuals must harbor an intrinsic motivation driven by a genuine internal desire for self-discovery, self-improvement, or fulfillment. A stark contrast is evident in the stories of Randy and Travis. Randy, motivated intrinsically, quit smoking immediately when faced with a religious conversion, finding greater meaning that surpassed his habit. In contrast, Travis, driven by extrinsic motivation tied to a necessary surgery, refused to quit smoking despite the potential relief from daily pain if he had surgery, showcasing the limitations of external influence in sustaining change. If you or your mate make changes for the other, identify what type of motivation you or your mate is doing it for to ensure it is long-lasting.

11. You are not sure what you want.

Understanding your desires is an evolving process, shaped by life's challenges and maturation. As you navigate through life, dating becomes a valuable tool for discerning personal preferences, dislikes, and deal-breakers. If uncertainty persists regarding what you truly want or if a specific person is the right fit, continue dating to gain clarity. Cultivate confidence and self-belief, allowing you to make informed decisions about your preferences and potential partners.

12. You are more worried about your wedding day than your marriage.

I have heard many of my students and clients discuss how much they have spent on their weddings. They wanted the perfect wedding day and did not care about the cost. Some parents mortgaged their homes to pay for their child's wedding. Sadly, some of these couples who had the perfect wedding ended their marriages. Spend as much, if not more, time and energy planning for your marriage as you do your wedding day. Instead of picturing the day, picture a successful relationship!

13. You are not financially ready.

The notion of waiting until achieving financial stability before marriage is a common refrain, yet the concept of being financially ready is subjective and ever-changing. Drawing from personal experience, my parents married with $8 in the bank. In some people's eyes, they had no business getting married. The difference was they loved each other and were committed to building a successful marriage rather than focusing on their financial status.

While financial challenges can stress relationships, entering a marriage with a willingness to work hard and overcome obstacles can be more valuable than waiting for an elusive state of financial stability. However, be transparent about financial situations, especially if facing significant debt or bankruptcy. Openly communicating and establishing clear expectations for both partners' financial contributions are essential to fostering a fair and sustainable partnership.

14. You are not emotionally mature.

Maturity is not solely determined by age, but rather by your actions and responses to life experiences. Emotional maturity, crucial for handling the challenges of marriage and life, is developed through experiences and how you navigate through them. Seeking professional or clergy guidance during courtship or when struggling with maturity is beneficial.

Marrying before the age of 25, when the brain fully develops, requires open communication and commitment since both partners are still maturing, with evolving interests, beliefs, and goals. Recognizing and addressing emotional maturity ensures a foundation for a healthier and more resilient relationship. In no way am I saying you should wait until you are 25, but be aware that there will be several changes that can happen to you during this time that could impact your relationship.

15. You do not want or are not ready for children.

Knowing if you want children, whether they be natural, adopted, or fostered, and how many, are conversations that should be discussed prior to marriage. Knowing what your mate wants is just as important. The following four scenarios show how different couples have worked through this topic:

- Neither Melvin nor Jean wanted children. Before marriage, they agreed that they would not have kids. Years later, they still do not want any and are happy with their relationship.

- Sebastian had no children and Melania did. He had always wanted kids, but she did not want any more. He married her anyway, but regrets that he will not have his own children.

+ Rebecca and Danny got married early and decided to wait for a few years to have children. They were pressured by family and friends to start a family, but stayed true to their decision.

+ Connie and Roger wanted kids but could never have them. Neither wanted to adopt, but after trying and failing to conceive, they adopted and now have children and are very happy.

Life does not go as expected, but understanding each other's perspective on these fifteen key points, and more, prior to marriage will help you prepare for your future together. While feelings may change, acknowledging that you cannot control your partner's actions is vital. Your locus of control centers on self-management; acceptance of your mate as they are now becomes paramount. Reflect on whether you are willing to wait for potential changes and consider what you will do if these changes never occur.

I learned a valuable lesson long ago—my desires do not automatically align with those of my partner. An unhealthy marriage often feels like running a marathon with a fifty-pound ball chained to one leg. As time passes, the race becomes more daunting, with the looming risk of collapsing from physical and emotional exhaustion. The key to a thriving marriage lies in mutual commitment—jointly identifying and addressing weaknesses and annoyances together to strengthen the relationship. Rather than allowing frustration to accumulate like a fifty-pound weight on your ankles, tackling problems as they arise helps keep the burden manageable. Neglecting these issues leads to increased frustration and challenges over time.

Choosing a spouse is akin to selecting a marathon companion. Just as marathon runners need preparation and familiarity with the course, understanding your partner and her intention is essential for a successful marriage.

MARRIAGE IS A SIGNIFICANT COMMITMENT

Honestly ask yourself, do you see yourself with this person five, ten, twenty, and even fifty years from now? Is she who you want to have children with? If not, why are you still with her? Make informed decisions, identify icebergs early, and prevent tough choices later.

When you are facing the tough choice to continue the relationship or break up, here is an analogy my dad gave me: imagine standing on the railroad tracks with both feet facing the direction of the train. The train represents the bad relationship. When you see it coming, are you going to jump off or let it run you over?

My divorce taught me the importance of addressing concerns and ensuring you know the significance of the choice you are making before committing to a long-term relationship. It is challenging to face the emotional turmoil of ending a commitment, so take time to answer the workbook exercises so you do not have to face the decision I did, especially after you have children.

ICEBERG INSIGHTS

Commitment in a relationship acts as the anchor that sustains its strength and longevity. Delving into the fifteen commitment reservation questions can assist in uncovering both partners' commitment levels and identifying hidden obstacles that need addressing. The iceberg analogy in this chapter focuses on the importance of building a solid foundation for commitment, fostering a deeper understanding of each other, and laying the groundwork for a resilient and fulfilling partnership. Before taking steps toward marriage, be sure you can wholeheartedly commit to your partner. Are you ready to commit, or is this still an iceberg you need to overcome?

CHAPTER 11

Get an Education

You can't acquire knowledge if you believe you already possess it.

CHARISSE WALKER

My entrance into college teaching was quite spontaneous—I was handed a textbook for a class and given two hours to prepare. Luckily, my degree was in the subject, so I familiarized myself with the chapter and prepared a lesson to fill the four-hour class. Before I walked into the class, I stood at the closed classroom door, paused, and faced a choice between two options: 1) admit my lack of teaching experience and preparation, or 2) stride in with confidence, as though I owned the room, and engage with the material I had prepared, I chose the latter. By the end of the first hour, I am sure if I lifted my arms I could have sprayed a firehose worth of sweat from my armpits from nervousness. The four hours quickly passed and the rest of the term went well and I was brought on full-time.

AT THE AGE OF TWENTY-TWO, teaching predominantly older, male-dominated classes, I could have easily been dismissed. However, my educational achievement and preparation earned me their respect and provided my basis to teach the class.

My formal education provided me with knowledge I needed to draw from while teaching several subjects at that college, opening doors I never thought possible, and enabling me fantastic professional opportunities, enduring relationships also require education and skills so we can not only open doors to new relationship opportunities, but also draw from them in times of trouble. Akin to preparing for a challenging climb, successful relationships require a combination of street smarts we learn from experience, and book smarts we learn from structured education.

Imagine preparing to hike Mount Everest with just a water bottle, a coat, a change of socks, and a map in your backpack. That simply is not enough and you most likely would not be successful. To summit this mountain, climbers are required to apply for a permit (proving they are physically fit), hire a Sherpa, purchase rescue insurance, and then bring the required supplies, clothing, and equipment. This list of items and preparation are book smarts, but it also takes physical, financial, mental, and emotional preparation, which are street smarts.

STREET SMARTS VS BOOK SMARTS

The goal of this chapter is to help you prepare for your symbolic hike up your partner's iceberg by teaching you book smarts that you can apply to your relationship and developing street smarts as you practice these skills. Some book smarts you will learn include understanding how socioeconomic status and personal insecurities impact your relationship. You will then explore why ongoing intellectual and emotional growth is important for a relationship. Lastly, you will receive techniques to navigate challenges you may face in a relationship.

Socioeconomic Status

A major hurdle that couples face is a difference in Socioeconomic status (SES). SES is a term used to describe your social status and economic well-being using three factors:

1. Income: the monetary resources you receive. This includes employment, investments, and other sources.
2. Education: this is your educational attainment, often measured by the highest level of education completed

3. Occupation: the type of work you hold in the workplace, and its prestige.

Since these are all interrelated, if you have higher levels of income, education, and occupational prestige, you are considered to have a higher socioeconomic status. If you have a lower income, little education, and a less prestigious job, you have a lower socioeconomic status. When partners come from differing SES levels they may face potential challenges in their relationship. Listed below are seven ways that SES levels cause challenges in your relationship. Visit www.flippingtheiceberg.com/chapters or go to Chapter 11 of your workbook for a more expansive explanation. Take time to identify how your SES levels can affect your relationship.

- *Access to Educational Opportunities and Attainment*
  Higher SES individuals often have better access to quality education, affecting the educational experiences and opportunities of both partners. In addition, SES status influences partners' levels of education, potentially impacting their intellectual compatibility.

- *Shared Values and Goals*
  Educational and cultural experiences often shape values, goals, and aspirations, which can vary between partners with different SES backgrounds.

- *Cultural and Social Differences*
  Educational backgrounds influence cultural references, experiences, and worldviews, potentially affecting partners' ability to relate to each other.

- *Financial Stress*
  Stress comes in many forms; from a desire to keep up status to wondering the next time they will eat. No matter the type of stress, it is relative to a person's situation.

- *Family Dynamics*
  Families have different values. When there is pressure to make money, sometimes there is less time for family. When money is not the focus, often family is.

- *Access to Resources*

  Although everyone has an opportunity to achieve whatever they desire, higher SES levels have access to more resources, which means individuals may not have to work as hard as others.

- *Communication and Intellectual Engagement*
  Education shapes communication styles and intellectual engagement. Those with similar educational and cultural backgrounds understand and relate to each other better. In contrast, partners with disparate educational levels might face challenges in fully understanding and connecting with each other's thoughts

Discover if your partner's SES level differs from yours. Recognize the unique strengths you each bring to the relationship and identify potential obstacles. Educate each other on your perspectives so you can work through potential concerns. Use open communication, empathy, and an increased awareness of each other's perspectives, to create common ground.

Identifying Insecurities

Jonathan and LuAnne were both established in their careers. Jonathan punched a clock at work then came home and enjoyed a simple life. He described himself as a country hick who loved the outdoors, dressed casual, and enjoyed the simplicities of life. LuAnne climbed the corporate ladder, where appearance mattered so her hair and nails were done and she dressed very stylishly, but at home, she loved being casual. She described herself as spontaneous, but engaged in self-improvement activities in her free time. Jonathan lived in a small, rented house, and LuAnne lived in a large home that she owned. They were dating for a month when LuAnne had Jonathan pick her up at her home. When Jonathan pulled, he looked at her home and mumbled to himself, "I can't afford her." Jonathan drew from his past experiences and believed that her lifestyle was out of his league. Despite his insecurities, they continued to date and as the relationship progressed, Jonathan shared his concerns with LuAnne. They discovered they shared similar beliefs and values and Jonathan found his initial insecurities were unfounded. Fortunately, Jonathan faced his insecurities and did not let them stop him from dating LuAnne, who eventually became his wife.

Unlike Jonathan, Carrie has not learned to confront her insecurities, leading to poor relationship choices and sabotaging positive prospects. After observing her dating history for several years and now single again, I spoke with her about her struggles in her past relationships. I asked, "Do you believe you deserve to date a good guy who has potential and a future, one who challenges you?" With hesitation and a hint of sheepishness, she replied, "Yes." This response unveiled a deeper truth—Carrie's fears led her to believe she was only deserving of partners who mistreated her, lacked ambition, or struggled with responsibility. The contrast between her verbal acknowledgment of wanting something better and her consistent poor choices points to the powerful influence of her insecurities on her decision-making in romantic matters.

Choosing companions with limited potential serves as a deliberate strategy, protecting her from committing to a lasting relationship. Further discussion revealed four primary fears:

1. fear of vulnerability and potential hurt;

2. fear of rejection by men at her level or higher;

3. fear that she is not smart enough or good enough to date successful men, and

4. fear of having a healthy relationship and being happy. Instead of rising to her potential and dating men who matched that level, she lowered her standards and dated men who aligned with her insecurities. This deliberate choice creates a barrier, shielding her from the vulnerability associated with a more enduring and meaningful connection and reinforcing a belief that she does not deserve a healthy relationship.

Addressing these insecurities and building self-confidence is a crucial step for her to break free from this pattern and open herself up to more fulfilling and positive relationships. Encouraging self-reflection, seeking support, and fostering a sense of self-worth contributes to personal growth and paves the way for healthier romantic connections.

Insecurities come in all forms: physical appearance, cultural background, financial status, spiritual beliefs, emotional well-being, spirituality, intellectual ability, professional accomplishments, and more. In the context of dating, individuals may be unaware of these insecurities or struggle with how to address them, leading to behaviors like short temper, emotional reactions, or quietness. Recognizing and acknowledging these insecurities is crucial for healthy relationships.

Recognizing that you deserve to date a good partner and that your partner equally deserves to date you establishes a foundation of mutual appreciation and respect. Finding someone who inspires and uplifts you might be intimidating, but the rewards make it worthwhile. Granting yourself permission to be with someone who fosters personal growth and radiates positive energy is an empowering choice. Surrounding yourselves with those you admire not only enhances your relationship but also propels both of you to higher levels than you might initially believe you cannot attain or deserve. The journey of finding and being with someone who mutually uplifts you is a shared privilege that adds depth and fulfillment to your relationship.

If you find yourself grappling with insecurities and fears, it is possible that you may not initially know how to overcome them. However, once you identify and acknowledge these insecurities, you gain clarity on what skills or knowledge you need to acquire to overcome them. It is a common misconception for some individuals to believe they are too old to learn new tricks, but the truth is, age is never a barrier to acquiring new skills.

Neglecting insecurities in a relationship can lead to detrimental outcomes, such as self-doubt, self-deprecation, or resorting to putting your partner down for personal relief—none of which contribute to a healthy dynamic. According to Nancy L. Johnston, unaddressed insecurities create fears of abandonment and inadequacy, adding stress to relationships.[64] When partners attempt to fix or heal each other, it results in frustration when they cannot alleviate their partner's insecurities. Embracing a mindset of continual self-education helps create a commitment to ongoing learning, allowing you to not only overcome insecurities, but also open doors to personal growth and development.

Importance of Personal Growth and Development

Applying this mindset to our relationships, choosing complacency in personal growth can stunt our progress and the progress of our relationships. Discover your partner's aspirations for the future, whether they involve formal education, pursuing a trade, or following personal dreams. Clearly communicate and declare your own goals, create action plans, and actively work towards accomplishing them. Without this intentional effort, relationships become stagnant, leading to a loss of connection, infidelity, or ending.

Differing attitudes towards learning and growth can create challenges. For instance, one partner finds enjoyment in hiking every day while the other is drawn to continuous learning through conferences and self-improvement. This stark difference in preferences, with one gravitating towards leisure and the other towards making an impact, may create a disconnect in their shared experiences. Finding common ground becomes a potential struggle, raising the possibility that one or both partners may seek companionship with individuals who align more closely with their respective values and goals. The key is not to advocate leaving, but to emphasize growing together—spiritually, intellectually, emotionally, professionally, physically, or socially.

Unfortunately, some partners become jealous when one tries to better themselves. These feelings poison the relationship. An example of how jealousy affects a partnership is seen in Jake and Jane. For years, Jake's attempts to improve his financial situation through education were met with Jane's guilt trips and negativity, ultimately sabotaging Jake's pursuits and contributing to the demise of their marriage. Regrettably, mates like Jane who allow jealousy and insecurities to overshadow their partner's aspirations can negatively impact the relationship. Look for red flags when dating to avoid a jealous and insecure mate.

Instead of dating a jealous person, find someone who is your champion. Encourage personal growth and development so that both of you continue to better yourselves instead of becoming stagnant. Wrestling with inner demons is challenging enough, and having a partner contribute to negativity rather than being your champion makes your journey both individually and together even more difficult. Offer support, encouragement, and be a cheerleader as you each pursue your dreams and face self-doubt. You deserve to accomplish your goals and dreams, surrounded by a supportive partner. Is your partner your champion, are you his?

Learning Relationship Skills

As a kid, I owned a ball-shaped toy that split in half; one side was blue, the other side was red, with a yellow handle on each end that had a whole bunch of shapes on both colors of the ball. The ball split in the middle and held several yellow shapes inside that matched the shapes on the ball. When I pulled the ball apart the yellow shapes came out. I then figured out which yellow shape matched the shape on the ball and put the shape back into the ball. If I could not find the shape on the side I was looking at, I rotated the ball until I found the shape and put the shape in the hole. I continued to do this activity until all the yellow shapes were inside the ball. I then opened the ball, dumped out the shapes, and repeated the activity.

Watching a toddler play with a similar toy, you will see that in the beginning, the toddler gets frustrated or loses interest in trying to match the shape to the hole. He may even give up, only to return to it later or the next day. After practice, he repeatedly finds the shapes and finishes the activity quickly, soon it becomes second nature.

Imagine the ball as your relationship, with each shape representing challenges you encounter, and the yellow shapes symbolizing the skills or techniques learned to address these issues. Much like my childhood toy, maintaining a healthy relationship involves continually learning new skills to cope with challenges. While you may have already acquired several shapes, the continual acquisition of new skills and techniques equips you to address a variety of situations. Using the same technique (shape) for every situation, or "hole," will not work. Gaining diverse skills allows you to build an arsenal of methods to draw from when facing difficult situations in your relationship.

Jared is one example of how a lack of skills to handle a situation impacted his life. His mother's method of punishing him was to use a branch (switch) from a tree. When he earned a spanking, she sent him outside to choose a tree branch, he then brought it inside, and she spanked him with it. One day, when he was sent outside to choose his punishment stick, his sister asked, "What are you doing?"

He replied, "Getting a switch."

She then asked, "You know Mom is going to hit you with that, right?"

He then said, "Yes."

His sister suggested, "Don't go back in, she'll forget in a few minutes and then you'll be off the hook."

When he tried that, he learned his sister was right! He was never hit with a switch again.

For years Jared thought it was normal to be swatted and that he deserved it so much that he got to pick out the branch that he would be punished with. In just one moment from his conversation with his sister, he learned a new skill. In most instances, it is not okay to defy your mom, but there are times when it is ok to deal with situations differently than normal. When you have a plethora of ideas, you have options to draw from and can get out of negative situations faster.

Jordan Turpin is another example of how education helped propel her family out of an abusive situation.[65] For years, she and her siblings were chained to their beds, allowed to shower once per year, strangled, beaten, starved, and more. Jordan found an old phone and started watching Justin Bieber videos when her parents were not home. She discovered that the outside world lived differently than her family. While secretly talking to someone she met online, she described how she and her siblings lived. The person told her the way they lived was not normal and she needed to call the police. That day she learned a different way of living, that she and her siblings needed help, and she now knew how to find it. Although it took two years to plan her escape, she saved her and her twelve siblings' lives.

In a relationship, you cannot predict the future and it is easy to have 20/20 hindsight. The more skills, preparation, and experience you have, the better you will maneuver through relationship challenges you face. Being educated about your spouse and having a desire to continually learn and grow are important. Each relationship is unique, and the skills needed vary based on your relationship. Regularly working on these skills and being committed to the growth and well-being of your relationship greatly contributes to its success. When it comes time to decide to marry, make an informed decision. Understanding who your partner is, what he values, what his desires are, acquiring skills you can both use in the relationship, and having the desire to grow together is critical to your future relationship success, so develop as many street and book smart skills as possible.

ICEBERG INSIGHTS

When hiking your iceberg, you need both book and street smarts because they provide you with various skills and perspectives to use when faced with relationship trials. For example, there will be situations where you will have difficulty agreeing. While dating, there will be times when perspectives may be deal breakers. Understanding these potential icebergs and developing skills to break the iceberg are key to saving your relationship.

In addition, continuing your education in both street and book smarts is important so you can draw from an arsenal of techniques that you will undoubtedly face in marriage. For your relationship to flourish you need to understand each other's goals, dreams, and aspirations. If left undiscussed, these become iceberg conflicts later in your relationship.

To acquire new skills, attend free community classes offered through school districts, read books, look online, or find a counselor, clergyman, or other trusted advisor. No matter what, get educated so you and your partner have tools to help you climb the flipped iceberg. Visit your workbook to further explore fifteen additional topics.

CHAPTER 12

Spot the Baggage

**"The heavier your 'emotional baggage' is, the harder
it becomes to carry, time to empty your bag."**

Charisse Walker

Seated on my motorcycle after completing the second weekend of my beginner motorcycle course, I nervously awaited my turn for my assessment, battling severe test anxiety. Despite flawlessly navigating turns and figure eights, and the finish line just thirty feet away, my test concluded abruptly as my bike screeched to a halt and the next thing I knew I was hitting the pavement with both knees, pinned under my motorcycle. Feelings of anger that I failed my test were quickly replaced with immense pain in my foot, knees, and hands.

I went to the emergency room where the doctor, after taking x-rays, assured me my foot was fine and insisted I walk on it prior to leaving. I protested, but eventually heeded his persistence. Rubbing salt in the wound, he triumphantly claimed, "See, I told you you could do it!" and left the room after directing me to see a podiatrist on Monday.

Monday came with no change in pain. Urgently seeking medical attention, I dismissed the podiatrist suggestion and contacted numerous orthopedic doctors until finding one available for an immediate appointment. After confirming my foot was indeed broken, the doctor applied a cast. Alarmed by swelling and circulation issues a week later, and the dismissal of my situation by that doctor, I consulted a third doctor, who removed the cast but dismissed my concerns. My foot was now turning purple from my knee down within seconds of my foot not being elevated. After showing doctor three what happened to my foot when I dangled it off the table, he was shocked and left the room after saying, "I don't know what else to do," never to return. Seeking further opinions, the fourth doctor, identified three fractures, marking the beginning of a lengthy eighteen-month journey of healing involving multiple treatments, tests, and months of recovery before regaining the ability to walk without pain or support.

THAT EXPERIENCE TAUGHT ME FIVE LESSONS:

1. Sometimes a simple and small event can break you.
2. You do not always see the effects of the situation right away, sometimes it takes time to see the actual break.
3. If someone says you are fine and dismisses you but you feel differently, keep fighting and get another opinion.
4. What works for most people may not work for you, so keep fighting and learn to trust yourself.
5. It takes time to heal from the break, but know that the trauma will not last forever and you can recover.

Just like my foot healed, with persistence, time, and the right help, so does trauma. After going through the exercises in Part I of the accompanying workbook, what might appear as a small childhood event of little consequence may reveal a much greater impact that has significantly affected your relationships and behavior in life. Since you have worked through your trauma, remember that your partner may not have. This chapter explores how the baggage your partner carries affects your relationship by expanding on the five lessons I learned with my foot now applied to relationships and past traumas.

Lesson 1: Sometimes a simple and small event can break you. Like a small fall on a bike broke my foot, sometimes known, or unknown emotional, physical, or mental trauma in your partner's past is creating a block that could break your relationship. In the beginning stage of a relationship, people often dismiss the red flags, or blocks, they see in their partners because they are enamored with their partner. After all, they are soulmates!

According to the National Child Traumatic Stress Network, children raised in environments lacking consistent safety and comfort may develop coping mechanisms for survival.[66] They become hypersensitive to others' moods, constantly observing and predicting the behaviors of the adults in their surroundings to cope with the day-to-day challenges. Trauma causes children to have physical and psychological pain, attachment and relationship issues, ineffective emotional responses, behavioral issues, poor self-concept, and dissociation.

Lesson 2: You do not always see the effects of the situation right away, sometimes it takes time to see the actual break. We all have baggage that we carry with us into a relationship. Just as the doctors did not realize the extent of my foot injury for months, the extent of the trauma we experience might not be known for years. Despite memory suppression, eventually the trauma will manifest. Taking time to work through our emotions and traumatic situations will help us identify triggers that can impact future relationships. The difference between successful and failed relationships includes how we deal with our baggage. We need to have open communication, support, trust, and love for our relationship to be successful.

Lesson 3: If someone says you are fine and dismisses you but you feel differently, keep fighting and get another opinion. Sometimes you may get help and other people think you are fine, but listen to your emotions and body, are you fine? If not, keep pushing until you find what you need to heal. As a child, Tammy's family moved to a new home where there were several children her age and very friendly neighbors. She and her siblings quickly made friends with all the neighborhood kids, and they ran from house to house, playing. Bob was the jolly old neighborhood man who loved having the kids over and he spoiled them with homemade toys and candy. His gifts eventually came with expectations. A few years later Tammy's family moved away, and Tammy had a very successful school life. Tammy began having flashbacks to her time with Bob and spoke up, but she was dismissed.

Out of college, she got her first job where after a month of working there her boss pronounced his love for her. Unable to stand up to him, Tammy eventually quit. In preceding jobs, Tammy faced continual sexual harassment. Her marriage was also troubled and eventually ended in divorce.

Lesson 4: What works for most people may not work for you, so keep fighting and learn to trust yourself. Unfortunately, stories like Tammy's are all too common, but Tammy sought help from numerous counselors which did not help her, but she kept searching and found what she needed to heal. Tammy learned that her inability to stand up for herself with men and the dissolution of her marriage was related to what happened with Bob. Now healthy, Tammy remarried, had children, and can tell her boss or colleagues no when advances come. When you keep searching for help, you will find what you need.

Lesson 5: It takes time to heal from the break, but know that the trauma will not last forever and you can recover. Although it may take years to heal, it can happen. Emotional trauma includes feelings of inadequacy, insecurity, lack of safety, and more. Will is an example of the effects of trauma in a relationship. He divorced because his wife cheated on him numerous times. Due to his experience in his first marriage, he became jealous, controlling, and hyper-protective in future relationships. He feared his girlfriend would cheat on him like his wife did. In addition, his ex-wife physically beat him so he had low self-esteem, lacked confidence, and was emotionally guarded. For years, he was in superficial relationships that provided physical fulfillment, but did not let women get close to him. He often engaged in online discussions to avoid real relationships. This led to loneliness and superficial relationships. Once Will identified his baggage, with determination and desire, he worked through his trauma and was finally ready to get close to someone, and found his wife soon after; it can happen to you too.

OVERCOME BAGGAGE

To overcome baggage, Wendy Lu provides ten recommendations to help potentially doomed relationships. These steps include the following:[67]

1. Communicate

Navigating conflicts in a relationship requires mastering effective communication as the newness of the relationship fades. Engage in open, honest, and consistent conversations, understanding each other's triggers and sensitivities without resorting to attacks or taking things personally. Explore past relationship experiences, desires, and needs. For instance, when Julie expresses a desire for a more serious relationship, and Jaron reveals he is not ready, they navigate the conversation openly. Julie, understanding it is not about her, builds trust by accepting his explanation. Through continued openness and honesty, they develop strong communication skills, eventually leading to Jaron becoming vulnerable to Julie. If you have ever been in a relationship where you tried like this, trying everything to get your partner to acknowledge you? The issue may not be you; instead, your partner is likely working through his own issues.

2. Watch for Patterns

One partner may be hypersensitive to situations, pick fights, compare previous relationships, become easily angry, or more. Watch for how your partner reacts to different situations and identify repeated actions or words. Does your partner act differently around family, coworkers, or friends than with you? Does he have road rage? Does he get easily frustrated and angry at the small things? Kyle acts very kind and generous to his work colleagues and family, but to his girlfriend, Sharon, he is rude, mean, and demeaning. She noticed he did this when he was feeling stressed or insecure. After talking with Sharon, he realized he was bringing his baggage into their relationship. Identify patterns and triggers in your partner.

3. Give It Time and Understanding

Take time to get to know each other. If your partner is honestly trying, then be patient and do not focus on her past. For example, Joe admitted that he was addicted to pornography and was inappropriately texting other girls while they were dating but told Amelia he stopped. Amelia felt cheated on, lied to, hurt, insecure, and confused. Amelia loves him and does not want to end the relationship, but needs time to overcome the betrayal she feels. To prove he is no longer engaging in that behavior, Joe grants her full access to his phone any time she needs to feel reassured. It took months, but Amelia found peace through Joe's reassurance and patience. If you feel your partner is worth fighting for, then identify common ground, be open, honest, and fight! Give your partner time to experience and work through her emotions.

4. Be Honest

Lying in relationships is damaging. Not the "honey do I look fat?" "No" type lying, but deceptive lying. If you or your partner consistently tell white lies, figure out what the baggage is that is causing you to do this. The truth eventually comes out, and it is much harder to remember lies, so be honest. Being honest saves time, money, and energy. Discuss your expectations, intentions, and desires. Do not lie for fear of losing someone. If you lie, the results when the truth is revealed will be much worse. Through your honesty, decide if you want to move forward after you have shared your deep secrets.

5. Be Positive

It is easy to be negative and attack each other, especially if you are fighting or feeling insecure. During these times focus on the positive and find things to be grateful for with each other. If you choose to stay together, even after the baggage has been revealed, then keep it in the past and start fresh with your relationship. Sabrina grew up in a critical home and Jeremy grew up in a happy home. In their relationship, when Jeremy messed up, Sabrina continually brought up his mistakes. Because Sabrina was used to being criticized, she could not stop attacking Jeremy since she felt insecure about herself. When you point out negativity, make sure to follow it with positive comments as well. Consider starting out with positive traits before discussing negative things. In addition, choose your battles. If you choose to fight over everything, even the small stuff, your relationship will struggle. Think long-term, is the concern worth bringing up?

6. Listen to Your Partner

Do not make assumptions and interrupt. Listen to each other, both verbally and nonverbally. Sometimes it is hard to have the courage to discuss emotions, so if your partner shows vulnerability, listen! Ask each other questions so you understand perspectives. Allow for expressing feelings and emotions so you gain insight with each other. If your partner dismisses you, this is a red flag and will only get worse.

7. Be Empathetic

Put yourself in her shoes and have her do the same. Figure out why she feels the way she does. Instead of minimizing feelings, validate her.

Wanda could not get close to Warren. When Wanda was finally feeling secure enough to tell Warren about what happened in her childhood, he understood and comforted her. Eventually Wanda trusted him and opened up more. Partners need to feel like they can talk about anything. If she is holding back, there might be a reason that needs further investigation.

8. Decide If You Should Have Couples Therapy

Sometimes an outside perspective can help you reach an agreement. If both of you want to work things out and you see a future together but cannot come to agreements on certain things that could be dealbreakers, then counseling might help as they provide a neutral perspective or teach new skills to use in the situation.

9. You Have Needs, Too

While dating, it is good to please your partner, but keep your independence. Continue to do things that keep you mentally, physically, spiritually, and emotionally happy. If your partner controls every part of your life and wants to be around you and do what he wants all the time, this is a red flag, figure out why he needs that control. Do not lose yourself in the relationship when you are not committed to marriage. Once you are married, this control could get worse. Reread Chapter 7 if you struggle with codependency.

10. Keep Your Commitment to Each Other

Continue to date to ensure your partner is someone you want to pursue exclusively. Once he is, then commit! Focus on the long-term objective and continue to analyze, validate, and enjoy your relationship, that is the whole purpose of courting. If your partner has trouble committing, figure out the emotional baggage that is preventing commitment.

Your mate's baggage may not be known or even remembered, so allow the relationship time, forgiveness, understanding, honesty, and empathy. Hopefully by acknowledging, accepting, and talking through the baggage, coming to agreements, and planning, you will identify if you want to stay in the relationship. Do not let either of your pasts destroy what could be the relationship that is meant to be! Baggage can be overcome, so allow the time needed to heal.

ICEBERG INSIGHTS

The iceberg must be discovered, acknowledged, and addressed or, like the Titanic, it could be what rips a hole in your relationship, causing water to come flowing in, sinking the relationship. Learning to identify the potential icebergs before they hit the ship is the goal of this chapter.

In this chapter, the iceberg is our partner's emotional baggage. Emotional baggage comes in various shapes and sizes and can be very damaging to a person's psyche. If left unresolved, the baggage your mate carries can affect their personality, how they handle conflict, react in situations, and how they treat you.

If you have not identified your partner's icebergs, be watchful and patient as he navigates the trauma and deals with it. Once you do identify it, decide if this baggage is too much to take on at the time. If it is, have the courage to return to base camp sooner than later.

CHAPTER 13

Set Your Expectations

Establish the standard for self-love, acceptance, commitment, and respect. Don't expect others to provide what you don't prioritize for yourself.

Charisse Walker

Jerry's parents were old! At least that is what his friends thought. His mom and dad were in their fifties. Jerry loved playing sports. At his games or competitions, his dad sat on the sidelines and yelled at him to do better. His teammates were all afraid of his dad. Jerry's mom was traditional and stayed home to care for the household. Jerry's dad did all the outside chores and supported the family financially. When his dad came home from work, he sat in his chair reading or watching TV until dinner was ready. Jerry helped his dad do yard work, but did not clean or cook. Neither parent was college-educated; his dad was a third-generation entrepreneur, and they lived in a town where everyone knew each other, few were college-educated, and most were poor, never traveled, and did not attend church.

Shari's parents were in their twenties when she was born. She lived in large cities her whole life where education was valued and expected. Her parents attended every game and supported her when she played. On Saturdays, her whole family woke up early, did yard work, then cleaned the house, and then relaxed for the rest of the day. Both of her parents worked, her family traveled to numerous states and countries, she had new clothes anytime she wanted, each child was given chores, cooked dinner once per week, and they were very religious.

When Jerry and Shari met at college, their relationship was like a Hollywood movie. They dated for a few months and then married over the summer. Jerry and Shari agreed that when they got married, they would be financially independent from their parents. They returned to college, both got jobs and took out student loans to support themselves.

After six months, Shari started spending money on new clothes, Jerry would not cook when Shari had class, so they ate out a lot, and money was tight. Shari asked Jerry to help with chores while she was at school, but Jerry refused. They started fighting about who was to clean, cook, do laundry, and how to spend their money. In addition, Shari went to church on Sundays and wanted Jerry to go with her, but he refused. On weekends, she watched her drama detective shows, while Jerry watched sports. On weekends, Shari wanted to go dancing while Jerry wanted to stay home. Their Hollywood blockbuster relationship was crumbling. Shari and Jerry wondered if they made a mistake marrying each other.

BEFORE CALLING IT QUITS, Shari and Jerry owe it to themselves to engage in open communication. Their commitment to each other deserves more than a hastily scripted Hollywood movie; it warrants the time to truly understand each other and establish clear expectations.

To avoid potential heartbreak, it is crucial to identify each other's expectations before tying the knot. Engage in discussions with your partner covering the following sixteen topics to ensure clarity on what you both anticipate from each other and the relationship. Many of these topics have already been addressed in previous chapters, reiterating the significance of establishing clear expectations. Additionally, the accompanying workbook offers more extensive discussions that I encourage you to explore.

EXPLORE EXPECTATIONS

1. Communication

Effective communication is the foundation for building trust, understanding, love, appreciation, affection, and a strong emotional connection between partners. If you learn to express your thoughts, feelings, needs, and desires more effectively, you will foster better empathy, compassion, gratitude, minimize misunderstandings and resentment, create a deeper bond, increase support and positivity, and establish a strong foundation for your relationship.

Imagine having a bad day and coming home and feeling like you can vent, knowing your partner welcomes you with open arms, comforts you, and provides love, support, and gratitude. On the other hand, couples who do not communicate effectively build anger, resentment, distrust, and annoyance.

Just as people are constantly evolving in their growth, so are relationships. Through this evolution, communication is essential so that each partner and the relationship effectively navigate life's transitions together. Both partners need to be open and communicate with each other, but establish expectations on how both of you will communicate.

2. Decision-Making

Learning to make decisions will either alienate or unite you in your relationship. Some individuals research, analyze, and critique a decision for weeks, or even months, while the other partner quickly decides and moves on. Establish expectations on how you will make decisions and what should be decided together versus individually.

Kyle was retired and went over to his buddy's house for a man's night. When he arrived, his friends asked him how he got his wife's permission to come hang out with them. He responded, "My wife and I decided long ago that we're not each other's children. She never asks me permission to do something or go somewhere, and neither do I. We agreed early on that just because we're married, we did not lose our adult card."

This gives both Kyle and his wife freedom to do what they want. He then clarified, "Now, out of respect, I'll ask her if we have anything going on, but if we do not, I tell her I am going to go do . . . and she then responds with, 'have fun!'"

They mutually respect each other and their time and space, and do not ask permission regarding how the other person spends their time.

Decision-making is influenced by the culture you were raised in. Some think that parents who make decisions together often have children who talk more with their partners. Others may think that children who observe parents sneaking behind each other's backs will often have a difficult time being open with their spouses. Still, others say single parents who learned to make all the decisions have children who are more independent and less trusting. No matter the situation or beliefs, find out how your partner was raised so you understand his background and its possible influence. Decide how you will make decisions together.

3. Emotional Support

Creating a sense of safety, security, understanding, and connection between partners is emotional support. We all want to be validated in how we feel. If your partner does not listen, acknowledge, or validate your feelings, then why are you with that person? Answer these questions, read the example, then discover how you or your partner would react.

> A. *Does your partner solve the problem or listen?* Some of my favorite mom moments are when my kids open up to me about their feelings. If I offered advice and solutions when they unloaded, how do you think they would respond? Do you think they would share

as much? What if I finished their sentence the way I thought they were going to explain it, how would they take it? Do you think they would come to me very often?

When talking about a problem, providing solutions or constructive feedback is not always the desired outcome. Sometimes, you or your partner just want to know you love them and will be there for them. They need to feel safe to express their thoughts and feelings, without being offered a solution, to know they will be validated and supported. If you are not sure, ask them what they are looking for so you both know what to expect.

B. *Would your partner rather be right or happy?* Imagine that your partner asks you to run an errand for her and you say you will. You have unexpected meetings, deal with angry customers, and come home to a mess in the house. You are tired and the last thing you want to do is make dinner and clean up. Your partner asks if you ran the errand for her and you tell her no. She blows up at you.

How do you respond? It is easy to snap back about how rough of a day you had and start to attack her, but how would that end? Instead, try validating her feelings. You could say, "You are right, I know I told you I would take care of this, and I did not. I am sorry. I know you were counting on me, and I was not able to get to it. Do you have a minute to hear how my day went? I'd love to explain why I did not get to it."

How would she respond? Would she be more receptive and apologize for getting upset? Try it. I have practiced this with family and clients, and it builds more support and appreciation in the relationship because you are reassuring and validating their feelings rather than being told they are wrong. Establish what each partner desires, sometimes one really does want to be right, no matter what.

C. *Does your partner give his full attention, including eye contact, when you are talking to him?* Imagine your boyfriend sitting on the couch watching his favorite sports team on TV. You come to him and start a conversation about what happened at work. You are upset, but the game is tied in overtime and it is a nail-biter. He says, "Uh huh" in the right places, but he is clearly not listening. He then cuts you off and asks you to wait for a few minutes. How would you feel?

Let us rewind and try this again. Imagine your boyfriend is sitting on the couch watching his favorite team on TV. You approach him and start talking about what happened at work. He pauses the TV and turns to you. He can tell you are upset, so he moves closer to you and holds your hand as you tell him the story. He nods his head as you talk, his facial expressions show he is empathizing and listening. How would you feel?

What if he responded, "Well, you should have . . ." or "Why didn't you . . ." as he tries to solve your problem? How would you receive his solutions?

What if he said, "I am so sorry you are upset, that sounds rough, what can I do for you?"

How would you feel then? Give him slack though, the game is in overtime, so you may need to be the patient one. How would he feel if you constantly interrupted him, knowing it could wait?

Showing genuine interest and giving your full attention means a lot more than "uh huhs." Providing emotional support and encouragement helps build a stronger bond just as easily as dismissing or solving it creates distance. These are differentiations that should be answered to establish effective communication.

D. *Is your mate your champion or cheerleader?* Years ago, I ran a half marathon. By mile ten I was tired and saw a group running, then walking, then running. I would pass them as they walked, they would sprint past me, then walk. This went on for over a mile. I debated in my head, "*They are walking and then running and are keeping up with me.*" I reevaluated my two goals and decided I was fine to walk. Boy was that a mistake! I hit what runners call "the wall" at mile marker eleven. When it was time for me to run again, I felt like lead was attached to my ankles. Mile twelve felt like an eternity. When I came through the canyon and saw my friends and family cheering me on, suddenly, I had more energy to run faster and to keep going. With the finish line in sight, I sprinted to the end and finished in a time that I was proud of.

As my family became my cheerleaders, it gave me the motivation and desire to keep going. I did not want to disappoint them, but rather make them proud. Did their encouragement of me start at mile thirteen? No, it started three months prior when I decided to run the half marathon. They supported my long hours of training by doing the cooking, cleaning, and babysitting while I ran.

Partners need encouragement and motivation in their job, at home, and in life. Do you support each other's dreams and goals? Find a mate who is your champion, not one who gets jealous of you and your success and sabotages you; establish expectations on what the support looks like.

E. *Does your partner understand you and love you for who you are?* As a mother, I have been through all the stages of adolescent life with children. The baby years are adorable and sweet, the teenage years they are figuring out life and what they want, and in the adult stage they think they know everything, and our advice is considered, but they still make their own decisions. I enjoy every stage of the experience EXCEPT the nine to ten-year-old stage because one minute they are happy, and the next minute they are face down on the floor bawling their eyes out. Confused by what I may or may not have said, or worse, how I may or may not have looked at them, I just hug or hold them until their emotions pass (possibly smiling or laughing silently). I understand they are going through changing hormones and do not understand what is happening.

Children are not the only ones who need flexibility and adaptability; so do we. We all experience different phases, moods, and emotions. How flexible is your partner with you when you do not feel like going out that night? Does he get mad at you and tell you to knock it off and come anyway? Or does he support you and say it is okay, and then spoil you rotten by rubbing your feet for two hours while you lay on the couch depressed? If you are wallowing in self-pity for longer than a day, does he tell you to get up and get moving?

Emotional support is an ongoing process in a relationship. Every situation is different, so learn the styles and responses your partner gives, communicate your desired reactions, and then decide if you are both okay with these expectations. If you do not, feelings of anger, resentment, and apathy will grow into what I call the Grand Canyon of divides that is hard to fill.

4. Trust and Honesty

Trust and honesty are the foundational elements to a successful relationship. To build trust, there must be open communication. Both partners need to be truthful and honest about their feelings, thoughts, experiences, concerns, and issues they are having with the other person. Trust and honesty build safety and reliability. If couples are not honest or trusting, then they are creating a relationship built on a foundation of lies and deceit.

Gordon called me while he was at work to tell me thank you. "Huh? Thank you for what?" I asked.

He said, "Thank you for trusting me."

Cautiously, I asked, "Okay, what spawned that?"

He recited a conversation he overheard between Olivia and Benny. Benny was cleaning out his car. While clearing out the trunk he found a black box that he did not recognize. He took out the box and opened it. Surprisingly, he found a GPS tracker. Benny said his wife was tracking him, trying to accuse him of having an affair. He shockingly recited the only places he goes were work, home, and to the store with her. However, she was rarely home during the day, was spending a lot of money, and he does not know what to do. Gordon said again, "Thank you."

I ask, "For what?"

He responds, "For trusting me."

I told him that I was not ever going to do that, and the time that I felt like I needed to, there would be a much bigger conversation that would occur. He agreed.

To build trust, some expect that involves keeping your word, promises, and vows. Gerald called Elaine out of the blue on his wedding day right before his wedding. After she congratulated him, he asked her if there was a chance between them. They never dated, nor was she interested in him, so she emphatically said no! She told him that if he was asking her that question, then he was not ready to get married, and it was not fair to his soon-to-be bride since he was not devoted to her. He got married anyway. It was no surprise when the marriage ended because they were both unfaithful to each other.

Once trust is broken in the relationship, it is difficult to trust in the next relationship. The phrase, "Once a cheater, always a cheater" is not true, but demonstrates a belief that people who are unfaithful in one relationship will be unfaithful in another. According to Robert Taibbi, the average affair only lasts six months to two years.[68] With only about five to seven percent of affairs resulting in marriage and a staggering 75 percent of marriages originating from affairs ending in divorce, couples engaging in extramarital relationships face grim statistics regarding the likelihood of a lasting union.[69]

Partners need to rely on and trust each other. Lies and deception have no place in a relationship. The other partner eventually finds out about the cheating and that leads to even bigger problems. While there are instances of love stories that originated as affairs lasting, a larger number of examples point to marriages that ultimately did not last. Just look at many Hollywood couples and politicians, although many marriages have lasted for decades, many more have ended, with some stars marrying seven or eight times.

One example of someone who defied the odds was Ben. He started a coaching business that required him to travel a lot. While discussing his extensive travel schedule with a colleague, Ben was advised to be cautious, citing infidelity being common with frequent travelers, ultimately leading to divorce. Heeding the advice, Ben took proactive measures and brought his brother along, even sharing a hotel room. Ben's commitment to his marriage was evident in his actions, and the strong bond within his family serves as an inspiration of devotion to his partner.

Once trust is violated, the ability to bounce back depends on how both partners respond to the breach. Recovering from past hurts can be a gradual process, especially when it comes to rebuilding trust in a relationship. People are prone to making mistakes, and imperfections are normal, but how we react to those mistakes shows our true self.

When your partner cheats on you while dating, this is much different than if you are married. Have an honest and difficult conversation with yourself and decide if the person you are dating is worth continuing to date. If she cheated on you while dating, do you think she will be committed to you in marriage? At this point you may want to take a step back and reconsider your options and take time away from each other.

The person who violated the trust needs to be patient with the other person and allow her time to move through the stages of grief: denial and then anger that it happened, mourn the loss of the old relationship, feeling foolish that they did not see it, bargain to get the partner to stop (if the partner has not yet), depression, and then acceptance. This process can take days, months, or even years to move through.

The proverbial phrase fool me once, shame on you; fool me twice, shame on me reflects the importance of learning from past mistakes while acknowledging the complexities of forgiveness in the context of deep emotional connections.

The way to speed up the process can be seen in Travis and Jane's relationship. Jane was upset and felt betrayed when she learned that Travis had been watching pornography on his phone. When Jane found out, they went to counseling. Jane was devastated by Travis's actions. As the months went by, Travis blurted out, "I said I was sorry! Why can't you move on?"

What Travis did not understand at the time was that he violated Jane's trust and he had to earn it back. Jane had permission from Travis to check his phone anytime she wanted. To show Jane he was serious, he put filters on all his social media and internet so he could not access it, and Travis attended counseling for his addiction. They also agreed that Travis would come talk to her if he was feeling a relapse. The two grew together and over time, Jane grew to trust him again, and Travis overcame his addiction.

I have heard so many relationships implode because of pornography. Both parties in a relationship must communicate with each other and tell the other how they are feeling. If Jane had gone through Travis's phone while he was sleeping and saw that he had been looking at pornography again, then the trust would be violated and they would have to start all over again, that is if Jane still wanted to continue the relationship.

Trust and honesty are ongoing efforts in a relationship. You cannot get too relaxed and think either of you are immune to losing trust. Consistent practice, open communication, and a commitment to integrity, no matter how hard, is essential to fostering trust and honesty. By working hard at these attributes, you can build a strong foundation. If there are any concerns, they should be addressed prior to marriage.

5. Values and Beliefs

Values and beliefs play a significant role in shaping a relationship and its dynamics. They represent principles and beliefs that influence a person's choices, priorities, and behaviors. Some values that need to be discussed include religion, marriage, children, family traditions and rituals, family principles, extended family dynamics, and career and work-life balance.

Religion can be a deal breaker for some, and for others it does not matter. Julie and Kenny grew up in the same religion and met at a religious school. They shared the same values and beliefs. Soon after they were married, they had children. Things seemed to be going great and Kenny was supporting the family while Julie stayed home with their children. Several years into the marriage Kenny decided that he no longer believed in their church and told her she had to choose between him or the church.

They both came into the marriage with the same beliefs. Each partner has the right to change their mind, but for Kenny to expect Julie to have to choose between her religion and her husband was an unfair request. Julie continued to love Kenny, and despite Kenny's request, he realized what his ultimatum was doing to Julie and accepted that she loved both her religion and him and did not make her choose.

Stan and Eliza came from different backgrounds. Stan came from a strict military family while Eliza came from a laid back, no-rules family. They met in college where Stan was excelling in difficult classes while Eliza took easy classes and was failing several. Stan was very regimented while Eliza wanted to enjoy life. They enjoyed dating because Stan brought structure while Eliza brought spontaneity, but the longer they dated they realized their values were very different and decided to end their relationship.

Your upbringing greatly impacts your adult life. Whether you agree 100 percent with your parents or not, you were still raised with their values and beliefs and these attributes influence your decisions and actions. If you feel like religion or your goals and values are not a big deal and you can overcome anything, take time to make counter arguments to your beliefs in case experiences change you. For example, if both of you are not religious, will you both be ok if one person becomes religious later and the other does not? Create what-if scenarios and talk through them. Discuss your beliefs and values and decide if your differences are too big of a hurdle to overcome.

6. Cohabitation

Cohabitation has increased while marriage rates have decreased over the past several years. In addition, marriage later in life is also increasing. Young adults are choosing to pursue careers, education, financial stability, and personal growth instead of marrying. They want more autonomy and independence than they feel marriage provides.

Numerous studies have explored the impact of cohabitation on marriage success, termed the *cohabitation effect*. According to Vuleta, couples who cohabitate before marriage are more likely to divorce, with a 51 percent higher likelihood for men and 54 percent for women in the first twenty years of marriage.[70]

Scott M. Stanley and Galena K. Rhoades highlight that currently, 70 percent of couples who live together before marriage now consider it a normal part of dating.[71] However, they argue that this practice is damaging to relationships and provide the following statistics for their argument:

- Forty-four percent wanted to spend more time with their partner; 23 percent of them divorced.

- Twenty-two percent said it made sense financially; 40 percent of them divorced.

- Seventeen percent said they wanted to test the relationship; approximately 33 percent of them divorced.

- Seventeen percent said it was inconvenient to live apart; 29 percent of them divorced.

Although Stanley and Rhoades believes that living together before marriage reduces your chances of a successful marriage, if you are considering living together prior to marriage, they give the following advice:

- Living together before marriage reduces your chances of a successful marriage.

- Take time and slow down. Follow the sequence: date, marry, then have sex.

- "Decide, do not slide." Do not drift into making unwise decisions, take control and decide instead of letting no decision be your decision.

- Do not take a *test drive* of your relationship by living together

- Do not move in together for financial reasons, especially to save money. Having someone bail you out financially is not the solution.

If you are living with your partner, ask yourself why you are not willing to commit to marriage first. Some questions, and more in your workbook, include: What are your hesitations about marriage? What are your intentions? What are your future plans? Do you both see yourself marrying each other?

If you are contemplating moving in together, think long-term and identify why. Cohabitation can cloud your thinking. Maintain clarity, and if you really love the person, wait. You will both appreciate each other and respect each other more. Avoid losing yourself in the process of trying to save a relationship.

I had clients who had been living together for a few years. They wanted to buy a home and the only way to do that due to their circumstances was to get married. Even though they had been together for a while, they did not want to commit to marriage, so they decided to stay in their current situation.

What does marriage mean to you? Is it important? If you are reading this book my hope is that it is. Marriage can work if both partners are willing to work at it and commit to make it work. However, with your partner, prior to living together, talk and decide why you prefer cohabitating rather than committing to marriage.

7. Children and Discipline

Children or no children. When you get married, it is natural for people to ask if you want children or when you plan to have children. This is a conversation that you should be asking each other midway into your relationship. I have known one person to want sixteen children while another person despises children and does not want any. If you marry someone who has eight siblings and those siblings each have between four and eight children and you do not like children, it may be difficult for you to be around that family, especially when they are close and find any excuse to be together. I have also seen someone who loves pets and wants a farm and no children, while the other person is highly allergic to several animals and does not want to have any animals in the home or yard, but wants children. I have also known a couple who try for years to have children and decide to adopt wheras another couple could not have children but did not want to adopt. No matter the preference, you both need to agree on whether you will have children or not, how many, if you want to adopt, or use a surrogate.

Roles with children in the relationship. If you choose to have children, understand they take a lot of time and energy. Decide how involved each person wants to be with diapers, feeding, homework, doctor visits, activities, school, etc. Open communication about parenting styles, decisions, responsibilities, and expectations is crucial. Flexibility and cooperation are also key.

How you will discipline. I know many families where the dad is very authoritative, so the mom becomes the nurturer of the children. I know other families where the parents have specific rules and are a united front with discipline. I know other families where the parents are non-existent with punishments or rules, and the children do whatever they want. Knowing how you will raise your children, discipline them, and teach them is so important to not only you and your spouse, but also your children. This should be thoroughly explored prior to marriage. How a partner talks and treats the children can have irreparable damage to the children's psyche later in life. Watch how your partner interacts with kids, discuss how you were both raised, identify what your likes and dislikes are, how your parents disciplined you and if you agree or want to change from your childhood. Even if you do not have kids yet, you should discuss how you plan to discipline your children. If you have not been around children, volunteer to watch friends, family, or neighborhood kids or help with community organizations to find out how you both respond, and do it more than once.

Birth Order. The birth order and family circumstances play into your discipline style. Although the birth order is a very complex subject that

I could write a book about, understand that whether you are a firstborn, middle child, youngest child, only daughter, only son, or have special needs siblings, these factors play into how you discipline and act with your children. It is worth taking time to explore. Or, sign up for a class with me at www.flippingtheiceberg.com/classes so you can understand how someone will react that you might never have predicted had you not been aware of the effects of the birth order.

8. Family Traditions, Rituals, and Holidays

Family traditions and rituals can be sticky conversations. My family has a very special Christmas Eve and Christmas traditions. As our family has grown and grandkids have been added, one of the traditions that is no longer followed by everyone is opening presents and not ripping the wrapping paper. The tradition started when my dad was a boy living in poverty. I remember when Gordon was first introduced to the tradition, it was very hard for him to sit through not ripping the paper because kids get excited and want to rip open the paper to get to the present. We compromised and altered the tradition, but it was sure fun to watch the reaction of my in-laws as the tradition played out.

Holidays. With holidays, is your spouse someone who wants to be with their family on every holiday and special occasion? Will you take turns going to each other's family homes, or do you not want to go to any family activities and celebrate your holidays alone? When one spouse insists on doing everything with her family and rarely goes to your family activities, will you be ok with this? What if you do not go to your partner's family activities? Decide now how you will handle these situations and understand that while dating you are still on your best behavior and trying to impress your partner, when you marry, your concerns and small red flags are exaggerated.

Birthdays. Another important tradition to discuss are birthdays. Some people do not celebrate birthdays, and other people make it a huge occasion that lasts one month. Expectations must be set so birthdays do not become filled with insults, disappointments, and resentment.

Extended Family. Family is important, but once a couple is together, how important is the extended family? In Genesis 2:24 it states, "Therefore shall a man leave his father and his mother, and shall cleave unto his wife: and they shall be one flesh."[72] Many marriages have been broken because one partner cannot put the other partner above his or her parents.

Kelly was married to Jim, and they had several children together. Kelly was estranged from her family and did not live close to them, but they did live close to Jim's parents and siblings. Every holiday and vacation were spent with Jim's family. Any time a special event came up, they did not have alone time because his family was always there. When Kelly talked to Jim about it, he dismissed her and told her to stop being a baby.

Kelly felt depressed, invalidated, lonely, and unimportant to Jim and she felt like Jim would choose his family over her anytime. No matter how much Kelly expressed her feelings to Jim, it did not matter.

Deciding how often you will spend holidays, vacations, special occasions, and weekends together are all conversations that need to be discussed and agreed upon prior to marriage. In addition, watch how much time your partner spends with her family while dating since actions while dating will be exaggerated later.

9. Respect

Jared would not stand up to his mom and would not defend Teresa when his mom or siblings spoke badly about her. By choosing not to defend his wife, Jared showed his family's opinion was more important than hers. It also sent a message to his family that he does not respect his wife enough to stand up for her, thus diminishing the respect his family has for her.

Because Teresa was frustrated constantly by Jared's lack of courage, she complained to her mom a lot. It is very easy to call your parents or siblings and complain about your spouse when you are frustrated. This is very damaging because your family loves and cares about you. Although you might work through the issues with your mate, your family does not see that, and instead is left carrying the negative baggage that you dumped in their lap. Henceforth, they think less of your partner.

Discuss how you will handle frustrations with each other and your extended families. Agree to follow what you decide. Determine who will be your outlet and follow through. Both Jared and Teresa are guilty of not putting each other first. It boils down to how you respect each other. Respect means something different to each person. One partner might think the tone of voice or time it takes to respond to questions means respect. Others are private and do not want their dirty laundry aired to others. Clarifying what respect means to each of you is important and you need to make sure that you both respect each other's requests.

10. Time

When Gordon and I were dating, we took a trip to Israel with his brother-in-law, Randy. There we met his sister and her husband who were living there. We made incredible memories on that trip and years later, Randy, Gordon, and I still refer to inside jokes that we created on that trip. Making memories together helps you grow closer. I once heard someone say making memories is more important than having possessions. Think about it, do you remember what you got from your sibling, parent, or partner five years ago for Christmas? If it was not a big, meaningful gift, then it most likely was not something you remember, but the trip you took you will remember.

While dating, the time you have together is precious since you are juggling work, school, sports, etc. and your relationship. This critical time should be spent getting to know your mate, so do not waste it sitting around watching TV or going to the movies. Instead, spend quality time communicating to understand, sharing experiences, building trust, and resolving conflict so you can decide as quickly as possible if you want to grow the relationship or extinguish it.

When you spend time together, you deepen your emotional connection by learning about your partner's feelings, thoughts, needs, and desires. This helps develop a greater bond and more trust. Take time to discuss each section in this chapter so you can uncover as much about each other as possible.

An example that portrays the importance of spending time together is Zoe and Jerry. Zoe was raised in a family where her parents did everything together. If they traveled, they did it together, and they spent every Saturday together, with or without the children. Jerry was raised in a family where his parents did very little together and his dad often went without his mom on trips. When Zoe and Jerry started dating, Jerry planned to go on a trip without Zoe. This was not a big deal until they were married and Jerry planned to go on a trip with his buddies without her. When kids came, Jerry chose not to go on family trips; instead, he went on trips with his friends. Zoe grew resentful because she could not understand why he would rather spend time with his friends than with her and their family.

Jerry's way to relax was going hiking, boating, or biking. On Saturdays, if he had a trip planned with his friends, he got up early in the morning to go hang out with them. If he did not have an activity planned with them, he slept in until noon, and then watched football all day. Zoe was hurt. She told him that she wished he would spend time with her and their family. Jerry said that he needed that opportunity to relax and that she was always welcome to come with him on his adventures. However, Zoe did not want to spend time with him and his friends, she wanted him to plan events and spend time with her and the family.

What was Zoe feeling and trying to say to Jerry? What was Jerry trying to say to Zoe? These are examples that happen in relationships constantly. How one's partner reacts to conflict will either help bring the relationship closer or cause more damage. If a partner does not take time to spend with the other person, they will grow apart. Sadly, Zoe and the family now prefer Jerry not come with them on trips because he gets angry and impatient. They now encourage him to spend time with his friends rather than with the family.

When I hear about relationships where couples cannot talk to each other after they have divorced, and they have kids together, it makes me sad. I am not referring to the extreme situations involving violence, abuse, criminal activity, etc., but rather the couples who have irreconcilable differences. How sad is it that these couples went from loving each other so much that they married and had kids and are now in a place where they are so angry with each other that the kids are caught in the middle. Spending quality time with a partner nurtures your relationship, protect that time so you do not grow apart.

Now, spending quality time with each other can be more important than quantity time. Quality includes being attentive, present, and engaged. Take time every day to sit down, face to face if possible, and ask each other three questions:

1. What is one good thing that happened today?
2. What is one thing you were disappointed about?
3. What do you look forward to?

One bonus question is what do you appreciate about your partner? It is also important to discuss concerns, and create an environment that you discuss feelings. When you start to feel like you cannot give your opinion, express that. People who implement this question time find significant benefit in their relationships.

11. Money

How do you value money? Finances are one of the biggest hurdles and stressors in a relationship. According to Rick Munster, 44 percent of divorcees admitted that before divorcing, they fought about finances.[73] The money discussion is not easy, but a must conversation prior to marriage.

After witnessing numerous relationships implode, I think this statistic is higher. If one person comes from a family that constantly spends money and is deeply in debt while the other person comes from a family where they had very little, these two people may have a hard time aligning their beliefs about how to spend money.

Diane was married to Don. Don loved to spend money and maxed out their credit cards regularly. Diane was the breadwinner, paid the bills, and regularly stressed about money. Don did not worry and often purchased things that he then hid so Diane would not find them until she saw the bill or found them. When she approached him, he denied it or lied about the purchase. When she asked why he lied, he told her it was because he did not want the lecture from her about spending money. This then led to stress, mistrust, anger, resentment, and so many other feelings. Is it worth being dishonest about finances?

I attended a workshop where they talked about spending money frivolously. This businessman said that every morning his assistant brought him his bank account statements and he figured out how to get the balance to zero. He advised people to not have a nest egg, not to pay off their house, rent instead of buy a home, and so many other ideas. However, he spent money to make more money. He advised against buying expensive cars, a home, toys, and eating out. I am sure many of us heard the opposite advice from parents, grandparents, and teachers, like pay off your home, do not go into debt, save for a rainy day, and go to college. Imagine if you had this man's belief about money while the person you dated believed in saving every penny, not going out unless it was free or you had a coupon, and you started dating seriously? Expect to have fights about money.

I knew a family whose child needed surgery. One of the parents put the surgery off until it was a certain time of season because the parent believed it would not cost as much during that season to have the surgery. If you were the other parent, would you be okay putting off a surgery and letting your child remain in pain with potential complications just to save money?

Another issue might be divergent financial goals. One spouse may want to save up as much as possible while the other one wants to travel the world. One might want to save for a home while the other one never wants to buy a home. One might live in the now with instant gratification while the other wants to save for retirement and live on a budget. There must be compromise and discussion about money so that both people have aligned goals.

Few people plan for the unexpected, but what happens if one loses a job, is sued, has a major health crisis, or dies? A plan should be in place. You cannot foresee the future, but you can plan for it. Prior to getting into a long-term relationship, I cannot stress enough the importance of discussing finances. Once you understand each other's perspectives, you can then establish shared financial goals and develop a mutually agreed-upon financial plan. Finding an honest and helpful financial advisor, creating a budget, or talking to a couple's therapist may be needed to get through this hurdle. I also suggest you talk with your parents and other couples who have been married a while to see what they do. Take notes about what worked and what did not work so you can get as many ideas as possible of what to do or not do, then decide together how you will manage your money together.

12. Combine Finances or Keep Them Divided?

Do you plan to have a joint bank account or keep separate bank accounts? There are just as many varying opinions about this as there is about how to spend money. I know a lot of couples who decided to operate out of a joint account when they got married. All the money that is earned goes into one account, and all the bills are paid out of one account. It is easy to track what comes in and what goes out that way.

One potential issue stemming from shared accounts is income inequality. Early in the relationship, openly discuss each other's financial expectations, considering the influence of individual backgrounds. Varied upbringing scenarios, such as one partner having a parent stay at home while the other had both parents working, or differing work arrangements, may shape expectations. Determining roles for each spouse is vital. If there is an income disparity, challenges may arise, with the higher-earning spouse feeling burdened, resentful, or superior, while the lower-earning one may feel inferior or dependent. Other couples may expect that and the breadwinner takes pride in supporting the family. No matter the situation, having all the money go into one account provides full disclosure and trust with both partners. If you both agree on the roles in your partnership and you both feel comfortable, then great! It does not matter who provides the money or who cares for the family, what is important is that you agree.

I have spent most of my adult life being the breadwinner, although I still contribute, I am no longer the sole breadwinner. Since we were married, Gordon has worked a W-2 job and both of our income goes into the same account. He has given all he has earned to raising our family, including his four step-children, and we are very grateful to him. While out of town at a conference, I sent my husband a text that said, "Thank you for providing for our family."

He responded, "It is my honor." I was amazed at his response and even more proud and grateful that he is my husband and willingly sacrifices for our family. Knowing how each partner feels about the financial role each one plays is important.

Not every couple likes this method for finances, I know several couples who said having separate checking accounts saved their marriage. One person pays the mortgage payment while the other person pays utilities, groceries, and other house-related items. If both partners are clear on their financial obligations and agree, this works well too.

When you are getting serious in the relationship, you should discuss finances. If one partner is hesitant, that is a red flag and you need to find out the motivation for nondisclosure by your partner.

13. Partner Roles

Expectations for roles in a marriage vary widely and are affected by cultural, societal, familial, and personal factors. Prior to marrying, discuss what your expectations will be for each other and what role you will each play. There are some common expectations that many partners have, but these expectations can evolve over time depending on what is happening with each partner.

Discuss who will clean, cook, do yardwork, repairs, care for the pets, laundry, etc. Knowing how you each feel about each activity is important before getting married. Fair distribution of chores prevents conflict, but that might look different for each couple, so adjust the responsibilities based on each other's strengths, preferences, and workloads.

When dating, it is natural for couples to want to spend all their time together. As a result, both partners are more willing to do things they would not normally do to impress or spend time with the other. I hear husbands and wives complain that their spouses changed when they got married. They used to do dishes, cook, or help with yardwork and now they do nothing. What changed? Nothing. The difference is that the real person came out and they are no longer trying to impress their bride or groom and spend all their time together or impress each other. While courting, observe how they act around their family. What responsibilities does his mom or dad have at home? Most likely the way the parents act will be replicated by your mate, so take notice of the parents' behavior and roles.

Communicating your feelings and thoughts fosters a sense of collaboration towards shared success. Recognize that roles and balance of duties may shift due to factors like illness, school, or travel. Equality and fairness do not imply identical treatment or erasing differences between both of you; instead, they involve equal respect, opportunities, and consideration for your unique qualities, abilities, preferences, interests, priorities, and circumstances. Attaining equality and fairness in a relationship necessitates continual communication, empathy, flexibility, readiness to adapt to changing circumstances, and a commitment to mutual growth and understanding. Striking a balance in contributions and managing expectations is crucial for cultivating a healthy relationship. Regularly revisiting and reassessing expectations ensures ongoing growth and commitment to each other.

14. Seeing the Value and Equality in Each Other

Valuing equality and fairness means striving for a balanced distribution of responsibilities, decision-making power, and resources. It involves recognizing and appreciating each other's contributions and treating each other with fairness and justice.

On April 15, 1912, the Titanic, termed the "unsinkable ship," sank in less than three hours. There were over 2,200 passengers on board and tragically, two-thirds of the passengers perished. The discrepancy between survivors and those who died were affected by a passenger's sex, age, and class. Surprisingly, only 20 percent of the men survived while 74 percent of the women survived.[74]

As a sociologist, I could hypothesize about why and what happened in this tragic event, but one easy explanation may be that the women higher up on the ship were closer to the boats and boarded first, whereas the women in third class took longer to get to the boats. In addition, men were chivalrous and believed in sacrificing themselves to save the women and children.

We are taught as a youth the importance of gender roles. The first question to a pregnant woman is, "Is it a boy or a girl?" Truthfully, does it really matter? Traditional roles were that males were the breadwinners while females were the nurturers. Times have changed, but due to these deeply-rooted cultural beliefs, being male or female impacts people's lives individually and socially.

When I used to run colleges, I experienced gender inequality first-hand. According to the US Department of Labor, women are paid 87.3 percent of what men are, and the pay of those with disabilities and minorities is a bigger discrepancy.[75] How does your future partner view your role? Are you inferior, superior, or equal? Do you believe that you are just as talented and capable as your partner?

Another crucial characteristic is to balance the power dynamics in your relationship. Be careful not to exert excessive control or dominance over your partner and vice versa. I have seen many couples decide that one spouse will work while the spouse stays home to care for the home and children. Oftentimes, the working spouse takes control because he is bringing home the money, and therefore makes the decisions. That is the point of discussing your roles prior to marriage so you agree on who will do what.

Having the opportunity to be both the breadwinner and the stay-at-home mom, I testify that the stress level and emotional satisfaction of working outside the home is much different and has a quicker payoff than working inside the home. I have heard story after story from students and employees who feel like they were looked down upon because they chose to stay home and care for the kids. In my experience, it is much harder to be the caretaker at home than it is to be the breadwinner. However, in many divorces, the breadwinner wants to take everything and pay for very little because they "earned it," while the person who stayed home and ensured the house and kids were cared for, the meals were cooked, and the bills were paid should get nothing. Although this book is advocating how to stay married, these gender role beliefs exist and are important to discover while dating.

15. Goals, Dreams, Aspirations, and Self-Improvement

To have a healthy relationship, support each other's goals, dreams, aspirations, and desire for self-improvement, which involves encouraging personal growth while nurturing the relationship. This is discussed in depth in Chapter 11.

Career paths are important to each person and can change over time. For example, starting out, you work while your husband finishes school. Maybe you enjoy working and your wife does not, or she has a better professional path and it would not make sense for you to work because daycare costs are about the same as what you earn, so you stay home to care for the children. Knowing the roles and agreements before and during marriage is what is important. You each have expectations regarding career ambitions and personal growth. Supporting each other's aspirations is important. Balancing career goals with family needs may require compromise and understanding.

Karl finds contentment in spending hours immersed in nature, indulging in activities like hunting, fishing, or camping every day. His job satisfaction comes from showing up, excelling, and clocking out without aspirations for management or promotions. On the other hand, Betty is driven to climb the corporate ladder. Devoting long hours to her goals, she could endlessly work. Despite these differences, they respect each other's space while ensuring they make time for one another. Once you develop your plan, revisit and adjust it as needed; it is not written in stone. If one of you wants to change your focus or purpose, talk through your decision.

16. Intimacy and Affection

You get married for various reasons, but some include a desire for intimacy and affection, both emotional and physical. Communication about each other's needs, desires, and expectations is crucial. Both partners need to understand the other when it comes to intimacy versus affection so you both feel safe, secure, and important to each other. When a relationship is new, it is common for two people to show affection by cuddling, kissing, or holding hands. This releases the "love hormone," oxytocin, which creates feelings of closeness and attachment. If one partner is not as affectionate as the other, the affectionate partner might feel rejected and look elsewhere for that affection.

Depending on the history of one of the partners, affection might be difficult for them. On the other hand, it might cause them to be too affectionate, that is why it is imperative you understand your history and deal with your trauma, especially before you are intimate with someone. Knowing the history of your partner is also important as it plays a factor in their desire for intimacy.

Trust, intimacy, and security are very important in a relationship. How a person is treated directly affects their desire for intimacy. Reuben is a very affectionate guy. He loves to cuddle, kiss, and be intimate. Betty does too, but she is upset with Reuben. As a result, she will not kiss him, hold his hand, and is rarely intimate with him. Reuben wonders what is wrong, and instead of taking the time to make Betty feel secure in the relationship, he shames her for not giving him what he wants, pushing Betty away even more. Betty and Reuben need to discuss their feelings and work through their differences before they grow apart.

Intimacy helps reduce stress levels. Physical touch such as hugging or cuddling releases endorphins, which helps promote relaxation and alleviate stress. Think about someone you know who is upset and you hug them or even hold them and they calm down. Affection, even nonverbally connects two people and often allows the one upset to calm down.

When couples take time to prioritize intimacy and affection and communicate what they like and do not like, they have a longer, more lasting relationship. It is normal that early in a relationship you take time to let the other person know how much they mean to you in as many ways as possible. I was reminded of the truth of this during our move. I discovered a drawer and some boxes that had several notes and messages I left for my husband while we were dating and early in our marriage.

Unfortunately, after the newness wears off, the amount of expression of love, intimacy, and affection often subsides. The most important time to express your love and affection is after the honeymoon stage, when real love occurs. Do not stop dating and courting after you are married. In addition, do not think that your spouse will change after marriage. If they are not doing the little things for you now, they will not improve after you are married; if anything, it will get worse. Express your needs and wants while courting so you both meet each other's needs. If there are no changes after the discussion, understand it will not change, and may worsen. Are you willing to live with your partner's behavior?

When my husband came home from work one day, I greeted him and asked, "On a scale from one to ten, how full is your love bank?" He had no idea what I was asking him or why and was visibly nervous and uncomfortable because he was not sure how to respond, thinking I was getting ready to tell him bad news or trick him. When I explained why I was asking, he easily gave me a number. I then asked, what can I do to fill your love bank more? He responded and I went and did it immediately.

This was a vulnerable moment for me, but he was not ready to hear it, and did not know how to react because this was not something we had discussed before. Have regular and open conversations about desires, comfort levels, feelings, and ways to increase intimacy so you further deepen your relationship and fulfill your partner's needs. I understand that what I like and how I express my love to my husband may differ from how he wants to receive it. If I am someone who appreciates service and he appreciates time, I may want to spend my time cleaning the house when what he really needs is time together. Doing what your partner likes instead of what you like is important to increase the connection with your partner.

Times have changed and sexuality is more openly discussed than in previous decades. Your view on intimacy before marriage may differ from your partner's. Before getting too serious in a relationship, boundaries need to be drawn where each partner is aware of what is and is not acceptable to the other while dating. Ensuring that you respect your partner and her boundaries is essential to building trust and intimacy. If you cross these lines, it might be a point of contention and resentment or regret later in the relationship, which could ultimately affect intimacy when you are married.

For example, sharing a kiss in a relationship could mean very little to you, but a lot to your date. Discuss what intimacy means to you and your partner so you can respect each other's boundaries. Being vulnerable about intimacy can be intimidating or scarey, but learn how to communicate so you are both satisfied and comfortable.

This list of sixteen topics includes examples, ideas, and suggestions that should involve lengthy conversations between you and your future spouse. Take time to review each one of these sections and be honest with yourself and your partner. It will save you both a lot of heartache if you do the exercises and have the conversations. It is okay to seek out experienced, older couples you respect for advice, but remember that what works for them may not work for you. Decide what is important to you, and do not waffle on your dealbreakers! Dig deep into your beliefs. Identify what you agree and disagree with, and find compromises when possible. There might be things you will not or should not compromise on, but feel they are not worth ending your relationship over. Instead, you now know that it is one area you will have to give your partner space.

The moment you lower your expectations marks the beginning of an unhealthy relationship. You deserve to have the best and you deserve to get what you want. Do not allow anyone or anything to lower your expectations. Instead, find a mate who motivates you to be better, that makes you feel like you hit the jackpot. Enjoy the journey of exploration and be open to new paths.

ICEBERG INSIGHTS

This chapter is a critical chapter for spotting the potential icebergs in your mate and the relationship. Everything discussed in this section will impact the success of your marriage. I cannot stress the importance of flipping each iceberg so it becomes a mountain that you can now hike together.

If you are younger, you and your partner might say one thing, but not realize the opinions may be very different when the actual situation happens. If you are older, the truth may be hard to accept, and opinions may be hard to change, especially if you are smitten with your mate. This is the time to validate. That means you go on the hike with your partner and really explore each section in detail. Spend time with each other's family, friends, and anyone else you can so you can observe how your partner interacts with these people. If you see red flags, do not dismiss them; instead, honestly explore these paths until you are satisfied with what you discover, and earnestly decide if you are a good fit.

If you get through these sixteen icebergs and are still satisfied with what you find out, keep climbing the iceberg!

CHAPTER 14

Recognize Abuse

"Survivors of abuse develop a keen ability to anticipate others' moods, looks, and actions as a means of survival. The belief that compliance and agreeability lead to safety becomes ingrained, shaping our way of life."

CHARISSE WALKER

It was a scorching day outside as the sun beat through the house windows. Sally and her mother stood face-to-face in the dining room entrance, engaged in a heated argument; escalating the temperature of the room to exceed the sweltering conditions outside. Sally had just graduated from high school and told her mother to "^*#@ off." Sally's mother, shocked and hurt, slapped Sally across the face and presented two offers: apologize or move out. Tensions hung heavy in the air as seconds stretched into what felt like minutes. Sally and her mother, standing face-to-face, locked eyes, glaring at each other intensely. In a defiant move, Sally uttered an angry, "Well, bye!"

Without hesitation, she gathered her belongings, packed her car, and was on the road within the hour, headed to her sister's house where she moved in, permanently. With newfound freedom, Sally embraced her independence. Shortly thereafter, her roommates held a party where Sally met John. As a child, Sally felt isolated, angry, and sad in her home. As a result, she bullied her siblings at home, but at school she was outgoing, kind, and everyone loved her. In high school, when a boy showed interest in her, she clung to him, allowing her to escape her family life. It was no surprise that within a few months of meeting John, they married. Sally believed John was her hero and pathway to freedom. They moved away to college, and nine months later they welcomed their first child into the world. Sally was far from her parents, enjoying parenthood, and seemingly content with her new life.

However, the idyllic life quickly crumbled as the pressures of raising a child and managing finances became stressful. John's demeanor no longer exhibited the same loving and caring qualities as before. Instead, he belittled Sally, made derogatory comments about her weight, and called her lazy. Gradually, Sally's self-esteem plummeted as she internalized these negative messages.

With a job opportunity in another state, they quit college and relocated even further away from their families. Over the next few years, they welcomed several additional children into their family. While John initially found success in his jobs, they quickly unraveled, and he was repeatedly fired. John spent beyond their means, resulting in mounting bills, debt, and numerous repossessions. The person he appeared to be while dating was gone and the real John was revealed. Whenever Sally dared to address these concerns with John, he demeaned and belittled her even more.

This toxic dynamic progressively escalated, transitioning from verbal abuse to physical violence. Sally and the children became the targets of John's rage, enduring both physical and mental anguish. At first, Sally complied with anything he asked and did everything around the home, hoping he would change. After years of abuse, Sally realized things were only getting worse. Any attempt to defend herself or protect their children fueled John's aggression. Eventually, Sally summoned the strength to divorce John. Because Sally had dealt with years of emotional trauma and abuse, she needed time to heal. Unfortunately, she did not take the time to heal and jumped into another marriage, which was also difficult.

WHEN DATING, IT IS EASY TO BELIEVE that the person you are with is Mr. or Ms. Wonderful, often dismissing the warning signs. Because Sally jumped into both relationships, she did not see the common warning signs that led to her abusive relationships. My goal in this chapter is to equip you with the knowledge you need to identify these abusive signs, helping to avoid the relationship, if needed, and identify where you have vulnerabilities so you do not fall victim to a person's facade.

As you read the following stories, be aware of your responses. If you are in one of these types of relationships, it is easy to justify, downplay, or even deny you or your partner's behavior. Talk with a family member or loved one who is not afraid to tell you the truth about what they think of your mate. If you do not agree with them, do not negate it; ask more questions to see why they feel the way they do. Lastly, imagine your 19-year-old son or daughter dating someone like your mate. Would you be okay with them being treated the way you are? What would you say to them?

IDENTIFYING ABUSE

Take an unbiased observation of your mate's behavior, see how she acts around her family, coworkers, and friends, and see how her coworkers and friends act around her. Observe her temperament on her job. Does she quit or get fired frequently? Are the issues she experiences her fault or someone else's? Is she a serial victim to circumstance?

Victims of Abuse

To understand the prevalence of abuse, the National Coalition Against Domestic Violence (NCADV) has some startling statistics:[76]

- Ten million men and women are abused every year, which equates to twenty people every minute

- One in four women and one in seven men experience severe abuse in their relationship

+ Women aged eighteen to twenty-four are more likely to be abused intimately by their partner

+ One in five women and one in seventy-one men will experience rape in their lifetime

+ Approximately 34 percent of abused partners seek medical care when needed

You might think, abuse will never happen to me, but most people do not expect to find themselves in an abusive relationship. With only one third of victims reporting abuse and such a high number of abused victims, realize it can happen to you.

Research shows that individuals who are in detrimental or toxic relationships often experience significant physical and psychological distress. A study conducted by the National Domestic Violence Hotline (NDVH)[77] found that 81 percent of women who experienced physical and emotional abuse experienced post-traumatic stress disorder (PTSD) later. Abuse is prominent; do not dismiss or justify it. If you are experiencing abuse or have been a victim, speak up and seek help. If your partner was abused, the repercussions of abuse can surface in future relationships, making it important to address and overcome prior to entering another relationship.

Sylvia is another example of someone in an abusive relationship. She was an attractive woman who had a beautiful smile, gorgeous hair, was in great shape, and overall looked happy and confident. While dating, Grant was an amazing man, but once they got married, everything changed. At home, he was dominant and mean, but with friends, he acted like the sweetest, doting husband who everyone loved. Over time, Grant gradually manipulated her thoughts, emotions, and actions, eventually gaining control over her. To maintain the marriage, Sylvia complied with his requests and demands.

To survive, Sylvia hid food because Grant monitored and controlled when and what she ate. He consistently criticized her appearance and body and told her how to dress. He controlled their finances down to the last penny, giving her an allowance, and dictated her every move. She was not allowed to visit her family or do things with friends without his permission. He monitored her calls and texts on her cell phone, making her explain the long conversations or multiple texts to family or friends.

If she "misbehaved" while they were out with friends, he would physically punish her when they returned home, only to apologize later. When she finally left him, he threatened to take custody of their children. Now divorced, she started dating again, but found similar types of men. Fortunately, she identified her pattern of men she was attracted to, stopped dating while she received counseling, and took time to heal before entering another relationship.

Sally and Sylvia's stories are just two distressing instances of abusive relationships leading to another toxic relationship, which is regrettably all too prevalent today. I have talked to many students, employees, and clients who have told me similar stories. How do strong, confident, happy, and intelligent people like these two women fall victim to abusive relationships? The fact is that no one is immune. Whether someone has a strong personality, is intelligent, physically strong, or a high achiever, anyone can fall victim to abuse. The abuser often exploits the victim's strong characteristics by suggesting that their strong personality is to blame for the abuse, or that their independence and assertiveness make them difficult to deal with. Being in an abusive relationship does not reflect on a person's strength or character, and it is never the victim's fault.

Unfortunately, abusive relationships often begin as seemingly loving and healthy relationships. Over time, the abuser gradually exerts power and control over his partner through manipulation, coercion, and sometimes violence. Recall the frog and the boiling water story.

In case you are not familiar with it, the premise is that if you throw a frog into boiling water, it immediately jumps out. However, if you put a frog in water and slowly turn up the heat, it eventually boils to death (although there is debate regarding the truth of this experiment, it is still a good analogy). This is the same concept with relationships. If things gradually happen to you, you do not realize it because you slowly justify the behavior, and the knob to the heat is increased a little at a time. The largest concern for people in abusive relationships is they justify or downplay their situation. They may think they can handle the situation and regain control, or that it will improve over time, or justify the behavior and take the blame for it happening. That is why it is easy for someone on the outside of a relationship to say, "I would never do that!" or ask, "Why do you continue to stay?" And then find themselves in that situation and not understand how they got there.

Childhood Abuse and its Affects

Another reason some fall victim to abuse is a lack of awareness. In elementary school, students are taught to "Just Say No" to drugs, yet they receive little education on recognizing abuse and learning coping strategies. How many children attend school each day, unaware that abuse is not the norm? Instead, we are taught from an early age to be nice, to deescalate the situation, or ignore the behavior. But in a relationship, you cannot ignore it or it will continue.

Given the significant underreporting of cases, it is challenging to determine the exact number of occurrences. However, according to the National Children's Alliance[78], nearly 700,000 children in the United States experience some form of abuse each year, including neglect, sexual, physical, and emotional abuse. I estimate the actual number exceeds one million children. This statistic is important because numerous studies have shown that children in abusive relationships either choose abusive partners or become the abuser themselves.

The sad truth is that children do not get to decide their home surroundings. They are often subjected to the abuse because of the parent's decision to allow the behavior to continue, often because the parent lacks the skills to identify, handle, or solve abusive situations. If abuse occurs, abused children often develop shame, and self-blame have decreased self-esteem, have difficulty trusting, and experience depression, all resulting in decreased satisfaction in their future relationships.[79] To cope with trauma, victims may resort to drug or alcohol use or display negative behaviors as a way to escape from their inner thoughts. However, the study found that these children can heal if they have support.

Victims of past abuse, whether from a partner, sibling, parent, neighbor, or coworker, may not fully grasp the severity of their situation until they are no longer immersed in it. If you find yourself justifying your continued involvement in an abusive relationship when questioned by others, it can be a red flag indicating that you may be facing a significant issue. Please start by telling someone; if possible, someone outside of the situation that is trained on what to do.

Types of Abuse

In addition to the lack of awareness about abuse, numerous other factors lead individuals into abusive situations. Abuse takes various forms: physical, emotional, psychological, financial, or sexual. Many abusive situations occur through eight common tactics. These include gaslighting, manipulation, control, isolation, monitored behavior, restricted freedom, threats, and disregarded feelings. Each of these tactics are further explained. My hope is that by learning eight methods, you will recognize these signs and understand the importance of getting help. At the end of each section, use your workbook to answer the questions to see if you or your mate are a victim, or the abuser. (The following sections are written as if your partner is a male, this is for ease of writing only, the situations could easily be a female abuser.)

1. Gaslighting

Gaslighting is a manipulative tactic where the abuser undermines your perceptions, thoughts, and feelings, causing self-doubt by lying or concealing information. Originating from the 1938 play "Gas Light,"[80] it involves a husband deliberately driving his wife to question her sanity, lose her self-confidence, and question her own reality so he could rob her. Victims often feel paralyzed by fear, leading to compliance and prolonging toxic relationships. Victims of gaslighting often result in apathy, depression, and anxiety, reinforcing the abuser's control. If your partner engages in gaslighting, be cautious and seek help. If your partner shows genuine signs of remorse and a commitment to change, celebrate and have hope, but be cautious.

Questions: Does your partner make you think you are imagining things or distorting facts to make you doubt your own perception of reality? The abuser discourages your confidence, denies objective reality, and erodes your sense of truth. This enables the abuser to perpetuate verbal and physical abuse while you begin to question and rewrite your reality.

2. Manipulation

Manipulation happens when your partner uses tactics, behaviors, or strategies to control, influence, or exploit you, often at the expense of your mental health or autonomy. It erodes trust and well-being, and creates an unhealthy dynamic. Table 2 below lists the various types of manipulation, what tactics he uses, and why he does it.

Type of manipulation	Tactics	Purpose
Emotional Manipulation	Uses lies, confusion, exaggeration, guilt trips, emotional outbursts	Manipulate and control your emotions to get you to relent
Deception	Lying, hiding information, dishonesty	Manipulate and control your actions to get what he wants
Passive-Aggressive	Sarcasm, sulking, silent treatment, acting nice and then displaying negative feelings or resentment indirectly	Manipulate you to comply to get what he wants by making you feel bad
Withholding Affection, Attention, Intimacy	Physically starve you by not kissing, holding hands, hugging, touching, or being	Manipulate and control you by withholding until you give in.
Isolation	Cut you off from your friends and family by not being allowed to spend time with	Increase your dependence on him
Financial Manipulation	Controls the finances, exploits you, takes access away from bank accounts and credit cards, gives you an allowance	Take control of you so you are dependent on him
Love Bombing	Guilt trip, pouting, or showers you with an intense display of affection, praise, attention, or gifts, especially after he did something wrong in an attempt to apologize.	To overwhelm and emotionally manipulate you into feeling indebted or feel bad because he is sorry.

Questions: Does your partner guilt or shame you? Does he act kind in front of others, but display cruelty behind closed doors? Does he offer apologies only to repeat harmful behavior? Does he blame you for him losing control? Does he influence your thoughts or actions, leaving you feeling pressured to make decisions to avoid his anger? Does he display anger quickly, only to act like nothing happened moments later and make you feel bad for what happened? Does he promise he will change, only to repeat his behavior?

3. Control and Isolation

Control and isolation happen when your partner exerts power and influence over your thoughts, feelings, actions, or decisions. This behavior manifests in the following ways:

- Monitoring your activities, including phone, social media, location, and activities

- Dictating choices on what you eat, do, say, and how you dress or act

- Isolating you physically or emotionally by restricting contact with friends, family, or your support network to maintain dominance, often by moving far away from outside support, making it harder to maintain relationships

- Undermining your self-esteem and independence by belittling you and making you feel incapable of doing things without him

- Criticizing and demeaning you to erode your self-esteem, making you feel unworthy to have an outside relationship

- Using jealousy and accusations to force you to choose to be with him instead of with others

- Keeping you physically confined so you are not allowed to leave the home or engage in social activities

- Creating dependency by controlling your finances, vehicles, or other ways for you to access outside support

- Threatening, manipulating, or coercing you into not contacting other people out of fear of a negative consequence or reaction

Questions: Does your partner make decisions for you in the relationship? Do you feel afraid or compelled to make choices based on his potential reaction? Does he try to dictate how you should live your life, what decisions you should make, what you should eat, and undermine your feelings? Does he try to control how you spend your time or whom you talk with? Does he attempt to limit your interactions with friends or family when you want to spend time with them?

4. Monitored Behavior

Monitored behavior is a sign of jealousy, insecurity, and control. This is achieved by the abuser:

- Constantly checking your messages in social media, texts, or emails

- Tracking your location to see what you are doing and checking to see if you are where you claim to be

- Reading your diary or personal notes

- Installing surveillance cameras that include video or audio in your home, car, phone, or computer to monitor your activities without your knowledge.

- Reviewing financial transactions like bank statements, credit card bills, or financial transactions without your consent

- Monitoring your phone calls or conversations by listening in or recording conversations without permission, or standing outside of the room to hear

- Monitoring your keyboard strokes to see what you are typing or doing

Excessive monitoring erodes trust and privacy in a relationship, leading to feelings of discomfort, insecurity, and a lack of personal freedom. Trust is a crucial foundation, and constant monitoring indicates insecurities with your mate. Set boundaries, expect transparency and have mutual respect.

Questions: Does your partner invade your privacy by monitoring your social media, text messages, or calls without your consent? Does he question who you have been talking to and what you spoke about?

5. Restricted Freedom

Restricted freedom is when your partner limits your financial, behavioral, emotional, or physical freedom and autonomy. Additional restrictions involve imposing rules and regulations that dictate your behavior, choices, or daily activities.

Questions: Does he attempt to control how you spend your money, where you go, or how you spend your time? Are you only permitted to be away for a specific duration or visit certain places? Are you not allowed to leave at all?

6. Aggression or Threats

Aggression or threats in a relationship take various forms:

- Physical aggression includes hitting, pushing, slapping, or physically harming you in any way

- Property damage is used as a way to control or instill fear

- Blackmail involves revealing sensitive or embarrassing information about you to coerce you into compliance or silence

- Weapon intimidation involves displaying or brandishing weapons, even without direct physical harm, to intimidate or control you

- Stalking involves persistently following, tracking, or monitoring your movements, both online and offline, which leads to fear and insecurity

+ Suicide threats involve threatening self-harm or suicide as a way to manipulate or guilt-trip you into staying in the relationship or complying with his demands

+ Verbal threats include making explicit threats to harm you, your loved ones, or your property, instilling fear through words and intimidation

Such behavior is a clear violation that boundaries do not exist, that it is an unhealthy relationship, and is not acceptable.

Questions: Does your partner use verbal or physical aggression to intimidate you? Does he harm you if you do not comply with his demands or verbally belittle you when you do not do what he wants?

7. Disregarded Feelings

Disregarding your feelings in a relationship can manifest in various ways. This shows a lack of empathy or concern for your emotional well-being. Examples include:

+ Invalidating: minimizing or dismissing your emotions by saying you are overreacting, being too sensitive, throwing a tantrum, or invalidating your feelings.

+ Ignoring or neglecting: failing to provide emotional support or comfort when you are experiencing a difficult time

+ Deflecting blame: shifting the blame onto you when you express your feelings or concerns, making you feel responsible for the issues in a relationship

+ Giving the silent treatment: responding to your emotional expression with complete silence or emotional withdrawal, leaving you to feel unheard and isolated

+ Making light of serious issues: laughing off or making jokes about the important and serious matters that you care deeply about, showing a lack of respect for your feelings

+ Dismissing boundaries: ignoring or violating your stated boundaries and limits, showing a disregard for your personal comfort and well-being

+ Interrupting and talking over: consistently interrupting or talking over you when you are expressing your feelings or concerns, effectively silencing your voice

Your partner should be willing to listen, validate, and support you and your emotional needs.

Questions: Does he downplay or dismiss your emotions when you share them? Does he belittle or invalidate you, making you feel like your feelings or experiences are wrong or irrational?

No matter the method used, each tactic is designed to gain control over you. Once you find yourself in a relationship where abuse is present, it becomes challenging to leave because you often blame yourself for your abuser's actions. You may believe that if you changed your behavior, words, or actions, your abuser would not behave that way. Even more distressing, when your abusive boyfriend loses control, you often internalize the blame and believe it is your fault. It is not your fault. Do not succumb to the belief that it is.

If you notice such behavior while dating, consider turning away and running in the opposite direction. Genuine change requires awareness, acceptance, time, humility, and assistance. Be cautious since apparent changes require verification over time. Everyone deserves love and respect, and it is crucial not to tolerate or engage in behavior to the contrary. If the relationship proves toxic but you are willing to work on it, have an open discussion, seek help, and embrace forgiveness and humility. Mending broken relationships demands time and effort, with an awareness that old patterns may resurface. Understanding your responses and patterns to such behavior helps build a stronger foundation for meaningful connections.

If you have a desire to work things out, take advantage of calm times in the relationship. Agree on a buzzword that tells him you are feeling uncomfortable or losing control and you both need to take a time out to prevent any more conversation that could be detrimental to your relationship.

When you are feeling out of control due to his behavior, remember that the only behavior you can control is your own; no one can make you do or say something, nor do you have control over his emotions and reactions. When you get angry or anxious, your body releases adrenaline and cortisol to get ready for a fight or flight response. If you can get yourself, or him, to pause and relax, your parasympathetic nervous system takes over, reducing heart rate and lowering your blood pressure.[81] This process takes about twenty minutes. If the situation is such where you can escape for a time to allow him to gain control of his emotions, do it! If you are being physically abused to the point that you are being hurt, that is completely different and no time out should be taken, escape when possible, and get help immediately!

I have covered various tactics employed by abusers and how victims may rationalize such behavior. It is essential to recognize these patterns to protect yourself from manipulation and control. Prepare by establishing a plan so you know what to do if you encounter such situations. Acknowledge the validity of your feelings and experiences, recognizing that you deserve respect and kindness. Trust your instincts, and seek support from trusted friends, family, or professionals if you believe you are in an abusive relationship.

ICEBERG INSIGHTS

The iceberg here is abuse. Understanding what it is, recognizing the signs, and how to escape is essential. It is very common for abusers to put on a good front, so flipping the iceberg and exploring warning signs in your mate is critical. This may be more hidden, so climb high up your iceberg and look in the crevices to identify it. If you spot the signs and actions, do not rationalize or justify; instead, exit or give yourself space to evaluate the person and the relationship.

Sometimes the biggest red flag is selfishness or over gifting. Do things have to be his way or does he give you things with strings attached? Identify his motivation for his actions without asking him. Flip the iceberg to identify the red flags.

CHAPTER 15

Understand the Importance of Giving and Receiving

**"In the right relationship, love should be mutual—
giving and receiving. If it's one-sided, it may indicate
an imbalance or taking advantage of the other person."**

CHARISSE WALKER

I love roller coasters, particularly the kind where you get securely strapped in, leave the platform, and anxiously await the ride, experiencing the rhythmic vibration of the "tick, tick, tick" sound while ascending slowly. The momentary pause at the summit is exhilarating, only to be followed by a rapid descent down a hill, navigating sharp left and right turns. The journey continues with repeated ascents and descents, twists and turns, and even inversions, creating a thrilling experience of unpredictability. The sheer speed and uncertainty of what comes next contribute to the adrenaline-fueled joy of the ride.

RELATIONSHIPS CAN BE SYMBOLICALLY COMPARED to a roller coaster ride, characterized by ups and downs, occasional jolts from side to side, and moments of coming to a stop, only to embark on the ride once more. Like a roller coaster, relationships progress through five distinct phases, as outlined below.

Relationship Phases

1. Twitterpated Phase: Think of a relationship you had when you thought, "This could be the one." Remember the excitement of wanting to talk to or constantly be with her. You might have written her a note or sent her a text, video chat, video text, etc. Then you found any excuse to do nice things for her, so you bought her something, sent her flowers, left a note on her car, or helped her with anything. Before you knew it, you thought you were in love. The exhilaration, excitement, and desire to give to your partner is like going up the initial hill of the roller coaster. This is the Twitterpated Phase, full of excitement and anxiety, and lasts up to six months.

2. Enlightenment Phase: After three to six months, the newness wears off and you start to see through the rose-colored glasses. During this phase, you become aware of your partner's faults, but often dismiss your concerns. This is where you have been on the roller coaster ride and gone up and down a few times already, it is still exciting but you are settling in. This is the Enlightenment Phase and lasts from six months to two years.

3. Realization Phase: In this phase, you take your mate off the pedestal as you notice things you do not like or agree with. In fact, the things you enjoyed or liked about your mate might begin to annoy you. You may find yourself getting bored with your mate. The red flags that you noticed and dismissed in those early days, you now address. Conflict happens and you observe how you react to each other. This is the Realization Phase.

You are enjoying the relationship ride and upon reaching the platform and no line in sight, the ride operator gives you two choices: but at this point you may be feeling a bit queasy and must decide between two options: 1) you choose to disembark (end the relationship); or 2) you decide to ride again (continue the relationship). For some, the ride was thrilling enough that you continue, leading you to ride repeatedly, but for others, you get off after the first round and seek a different ride. In a relationship, you may enjoy this phase and want to continue, or you may be ready to move on. Take time to get to know each other and work through the nuances of the relationship.

4. Maneuver Phase: Similar to your relationship, you enjoy the twists and turns on the ride. This is when you realize you either have a lot in common and are on the ride for the long haul, or do not have as much in common, you do not agree with her values or ideals, or you do not like something else, so you choose to get off the ride after a few times. If you remained on, there were turns (conflicts and red flags) you do not like, but you worked through them and chose to stay on the ride. This phase is called the Maneuver Phase.

5. Sure Love Phase: If you stay on the ride you say, "This is awesome!" or "I love it!" as you continue. This is called the Sure Love Phase. You choose to commit to the relationship. Sure, you experienced the rocky, difficult, and surprising times, but the superficial relationship has passed and you overlook her faults because no matter what, you love and accept her for who she is and want to be with her.

The acronym for these phases spells **T.E.R.M.S.**, because just like the roller coaster, the relationship continues to go in circles (or terms). But if the relationship is sure love, you are willing to ride the roller coaster forever. The best way to continue good TERMS and ensure a lasting relationship is to keep serving each other. Just like the roller coaster, relationships are scary, hard, treacherous, and tough at times, but if you continually serve each other, your love will grow stronger.

I used to hear that a relationship can only survive if both people are working equally at it. I no longer agree with that. We all take turns on the roller coaster of life. When you are feeling low, your partner may be high, giving 100 percent so he can support and encourage you to get back up the hill. When he is low, this might be your time to give 100 percent effort into getting things done or caring for your loved one, knowing that he will eventually subsidize your effort in the relationship. Therefore, I highly recommend that you give enough time for a relationship to experience the ups and downs you will experience in life and the relationship before jumping in and committing after such little time. Get past the realization phase before choosing to commit to marriage.

Cause of Marriage Failure

If you were to ask any divorced couple the reason for their divorce, several partners would give one of these sixteen reasons:

- Financial (hiding, lacking, or having money)
- Intimacy preferences
- Constant arguing
- Desiring a change
- Growing Apart
- Addictions
- Extended family interference
- Differing expectations
- Lack of communication
- Spending excessive time on hobbies (like video games)
- Abuse (substance or domestic)
- Parenting conflicts
- Professional differences or goals
- Self-sabotage
- One person taking on all the responsibilities

There are other reasons, like health, but if the cause is one of the answers above, I sum all of these reasons into one word: selfishness.

Reflect for a moment on why couples choose to marry—the joy of spending time together, love, and mutual happiness. Initially, the couple is head over heels in love and happy. No matter what anyone says, they are going to get married, and do. Now, think about the financial investment they made for their wedding. It is disheartening to witness couples, after only one or two years, decide to end their marriage. Consider whether you would be willing to invest the same amount of money spent on your wedding to save your marriage and reignite the romance or work through your problems. If you are not willing to spend as much to save it, then why marry and spend all that money in the first place?

I am not downplaying the bad situations, but even those are selfish. Although this is a relationship book for single people, I want you to think about the reasons you may decide to end your relationship. Maybe your relationship has potential but one of these sixteen reasons is why it is coming to an end. Is it worth working through to continue the relationship? Review these sixteen reasons and explanations and see if your relationship is salvageable if you both choose to work through these concerns. Understand though, that these reasons will most likely be the reasons your marriage comes to an end in the future if you do not work through them.

1. Cheating. Are you being selfish and only thinking about yourself and your selfish desires?
2. Finances. Are you hiding things or spending beyond your means? This is selfish. If it is due to stress, are you doing everything you can to get out of it? If so, this does not fall under selfishness, but be honest, have you cut your spending or are you still eating out or spending on frivolous food, entertainment, or addictions?

3. Intimacy Preferences. Are you communicating with your partner? Is your partner willing to be open and experiment with you?

4. Constant arguing. Are you seeing each other's perspectives and working to understand?

5. Desiring a Change: It is easy to get tired of each other, but are you still dating each other and spending time with each other and focusing on the positive qualities or just the negative ones?

6. Growing Apart. this is similar to #5, how much time are you spending together? Start a hobby together, talk with each other, make time for each other.

7. Addictions. Although they are hard to break, are they more important than your spouse? You did not make a commitment to it, you made a commitment to your partner.

8. Extended Family Interference. Remember how your family told you not to get involved but you did anyway? Now is the time to tell them to back off, stand up to them, and give your partner the respect they deserve.

9. Differing Expectations. We all have expectations, but have you taken an inventory and decided if your expectations are realistic or not? Find common ground and communicate with each other.

10. Lack of Communication. Do you take time to communicate daily, talk about your fears, frustrations, likes, dislikes.

11. Spending Excessive Time on Hobbies. Are these becoming an addiction that takes your time away from each other? Is it improving yourself or are you just wasting time?

12. Abuse. Are you hurting others emotionally, physically, mentally? This is pure selfishness.

13. Parenting Conflicts. Although you do not always agree, are you a united front? Becoming a united front is important.

Constant communication and compromise are important. There is no place for belittling or attacking a child's confidence, but discipline varies and should be discussed.

14. Professional Differences or Goals. Although it is normal to not have the same ambitions and goals, but do you discuss your goals and support each other? Constant communication and making time for each other is critical. Is the relationship more important, or are your goals?

15. Self-Sabotage. Do you suffer from imposter syndrom and allow it to affect you? The whole purpose of Part I of this book was to work through your trauma. If you still have problems, continue to seek help and discuss your fears and insecurities that you are allowing to affect the relationship.

16. Unbalanced Share of Responsibilities. Is there equal share of responsibilities? Both partners need to be committed to helping each other. If you are allowing your mate to cook, clean, handle the finances, the children, and anything else while you watch television, play video games, or lay in bed, that is not fair to your partner.

As you can see above, when you stop putting your partner's needs above yours, that is selfishness, and often the explanation for the term, "irreconcilable differences" that is used in the divorce decree.

There are many negative feelings that selfishness causes in a relationship. This includes resentment, lack of collaboration, emotional distance, lack of trust and safety, diminished relationship satisfaction, frustration, anger, neglect, feeling disregarded, and resentment. When one partner feels like this, he becomes apathetic. If the other partner is focused on himself, then selfishness hinders effective collaboration and decision-making.

The partner who feels like he is not important may pull away and shut off from sharing his feelings, resulting in a lack of shared values and a strained relationship. The person who feels diminished or unimportant may emotionally detach or become apathetic. This results in loneliness and isolation. This is particularly sad because the person feeling lonely might look elsewhere, while the one being selfish may blame the other person for shutting off and finding satisfaction elsewhere, justifying that she is not getting what she needs from the relationship. Did you follow? If not, read it again.

The Importance of Charity and Service

The opposite of selfishness is charity. To understand the importance of charity, let us further explore an iceberg. Due to weather, situations, and animals, an iceberg is constantly changing. It both grows and shrinks as pieces of it chip off. These chips are called bergy-bits or growlers.[82] A bergy-bit has a more positive connotation while a growler has a more negative connotation. However, they mean the same thing. When talking to your partner, word choice can skew your mate's reaction, so make sure you frame the situation as positively as possible and choose your words wisely. The next time you need to address an iceberg that is affecting your relationship, use bergy-bit wording instead of growlers.

Getting back to the iceberg analogy, each time you give, you are creating a bergy-bit that floats down the water, leaving a piece of yourself as you interact with others. The amazing thing is that these little bits of broken-off ice become habitats for numerous wildlife that use them to gain strength, air, and rest before going back into or over the water. Often you see seals or penguins use the bergy-bits to rest from their journey. In addition, these pieces are known to nourish the ocean because over the years the iceberg accumulates nutrients from the air. When the iceberg melts or breaks off, the dust that has accumulated for hundreds of years is now free and used by phytoplankton as food, in turn, it becomes food for krill and zooplankton, initiating large hotspots to feed larger animals such as the great whales.[83] This chain reaction of ecological activity is fueled by the essential nutrients released from icebergs

Your experience is like the phytoplankton. What you have learned and given to others allows you to pay it forward just like the little pieces of ice now continuing to help the food chain progress. By serving your partner, you are not only helping him but also your relationship, as the law of reciprocation is implemented. This is where someone does something for you, you feel obligated to return the favor. In a relationship, if two people are serving each other, they are growing to love each other more. In a healthy relationship, giving and receiving happens often between partners.

Sloane Davidson[84] believed that by embracing the joy of giving today, what you get would come back to you tenfold. There are also Biblical references to God stating that what you give, you will be blessed for. Why is giving so important? Because when we give to others, we are showing that we care about others and we want them to be well. You have the power to be charitable, and you have the responsibility to make your relationship work (if it is not abusive).

I am sure you have heard the adage, "Giving is better than receiving." This has a Biblical reference to Acts 20:35[85] where Paul states, "It is more blessed to give than to receive." People who give of their time, talents, and money tend to be very different from those who do not. Why? Because when you take the time to serve people, you are not only spending time doing things for others, but also spending less time doing things for yourself. Service softens the heart, so when you serve, you learn from them and learn to love them.

The same applies to our relationship. Not everyone is born into the same socioeconomic status. Can anyone achieve what they want if they put their mind and effort into it? Yes. But does that mean that everyone has equal obstacles? Definitely not! When interviewing for jobs, you may have heard, "It doesn't matter what you know, but who you know."

This is true, but it is also possible to achieve what you want if you put enough time and effort into it. If you want to save your relationship, then put time and effort into it!

In relationships, it is easy to become the victim and feel like you are being wronged by your partner, I have been there, I get it. However, instead of being a victim, swallow your pride and start serving. There is a story titled, "30 Days of Carrying My Wife"[86] that has been spread around the internet for several years, with varying versions. The story is told from the husband's perspective.

One night he returns home after work and while eating dinner, he takes his wife's hand and asks for a divorce. The story then unfolds with the wife being shocked and responding that he is not a man. The husband is determined to proceed with the divorce and drafts an agreement, giving her the home, car, and 30 percent ownership of the company. She rips it up and two days later, presents her own divorce conditions. For 30 days he will do two things: 1) live normally so their son will not be upset by the news and can prepare for his tests, and 2) he will carry her from their bedroom to the front door every morning, just like he carried her into their bridal room the day of their marriage. Thinking it an odd request, but cheaper than his terms, he agreed.

Day one was a bit awkward, but when he did it, his son was excited and even clapped. Day two was still clumsy, but she laid on him and he smelled her perfume. By day four he began to intimately desire her. While carrying her, he remembered how she had given him everything he wanted and had been completely devoted to him. Day five and six his desire for intimacy grew stronger.

Soon the month was nearly over and his service toward her made him more aware of her. He noticed that she was more frail and thin than when he started the month. He was also impressed at how well she was accepting the breakup. As the weeks carried on, when he went to pick her up, he tenderly touched her head and their son began reminding his dad it was time to carry mom to the door, showing the impact service had on the entire family. When the husband picked her up, she put her arms around his neck.

By day 30, he realized the month was over, but instead of being happy, he could hardly take a step as he was filled with remorse and other emotions. This time he held her close and moved slowly towards the door. Realizing he still loved his wife, he regrettably put her down, hugged her and left. He drove to his mistress's home, ended the relationship, and told her he was staying with his wife.

He then drove to the florist to buy flowers. On the card, he wrote that he would carry her every morning until they die. He drove home, excited to greet his wife, give her the flowers, and tell her the news. He threw open the door, calling for his wife, but it was quiet. He ran to their bedroom where he saw her on the bed with her eyes closed. When he approached her, he realized she had passed away while he was saying goodbye to his mistress.

Unbeknownst to him, his wife had been fighting cancer for a few months. To protect her son from what could happen from divorce and knowing she was going to die, she made a simple, unselfish request that also protected her husband. This was an ultimate sacrifice and portrayal of unselfishness. She loved her family and did what she could to show that. In addition, because her husband was serving her, he fell in love with her again. What was amazing was that after only a few days his heart softened towards her, it does not take long if you have a desire to be vulnerable and sincere. I wonder how many relationships would turn around if more partners started serving their partners rather than thinking of themselves.

We are all blessed with different abilities and talents. Some of us are blessed with singing, drawing, speaking, creating, logical thinking, and so on. By sharing your talents with others, you are teaching, enriching, and helping them. I am so grateful to so many singers, like my son, for sharing their talents with me so I can have the feelings I do when I listen to their music. I have a daughter who creates magnificent works of art, especially religious. She has touched so many lives by recreating memories, thoughts, and feelings of our time together as well as religious pictures that evoke incredible emotions. I have another daughter who creates wonderful videos of our times together and creates activities for our family to spend time together. These are talents that are unique to them but bless our family.

There is a change that comes over people when they provide charity. Think of the last time you helped your partner. Did it leave you wanting to do more? When we give, we help not only our partner but also ourselves. It gets us outside of our comfort zone and makes an impact. When we help our partner, family, and others, we become better people.

A genuine giver's persona and attitude changes a person. Have you ever met people who are so easy to be around? They are happy, comfortable with who they are, and you feel so accepted when you are with them. Have you spent enough time with them and found that they are very giving of their time, energy, money, etc.?

A good example of how service changes people is Britt. She had a very difficult childhood and did not speak about her past, but because of her past, she was filled with significant insecurities and regret, which made her critical of others. As she served other people for years, the insecurities and regret she once felt were replaced with healing and love toward other people. Her heart was changed and she is happy, comfortable, loving, and anything but critical. It was an amazing transformation and she has blessed hundreds of people as a result. When we give to others, we are leaving a piece of ourselves with them, and our hearts are softened and even healed.

Giving is a meaningful expression of love, care, and generosity, involving the offering of time, attention, affection, and assistance to others. Through serving, we learn to love and accept people despite their flaws. However, it is crucial that giving is driven by a genuine desire rather than an obligation. When approached as an obligation, it leads to feelings of resentment, anger, or frustration.

The Importance of Receiving

In addition to the gratification that comes from giving, it is equally important to allow others to serve and support you. If you find fulfillment in acts of generosity, then provide the opportunity for your partner to experience that same sense of reward by allowing him to give to you.

Receiving requires vulnerability, openness, humility, and a readiness to embrace the support, kindness, and love offered by those around you. It is a reciprocal exchange that not only benefits you but also allows others to share in the joy of giving and contributing to your well-being.

You may struggle with feelings of unworthiness, fear, and pride, making it uncomfortable to receive. However, if you are consistently in a giving mode without allowing yourself to receive, you risk emptying your bucket before you have time to fill it, resulting in you having nothing else to give as your bucket has dried up.

In a relationship, if you are the sole giver and your partner does not reciprocate, it signals a potential issue of selfishness on her part. It could also indicate her insecurity, highlighting a need for guidance on how to give and receive to meet your needs. Much like a roller coaster, life brings highs and lows, presenting opportunities for mutual support and celebration.

For a thriving relationship, achieving balance in the give-and-take dynamic is crucial. Humility, communication, vulnerability, and a willingness to serve and be served contribute to a harmonious relationship. Discussing needs, desires, and boundaries fosters understanding.

In Gary Chapman's book, *The 5 Love Languages*, he offers insights into preferred ways of expressing and receiving love.[87] Recognizing each other's love language and catering to it contributes to a more fulfilling connection.

Expressing gratitude when served can be challenging, yet it is essential for maintaining the cycle of giving and receiving. This reciprocal exchange provides emotional intimacy, creating a secure space for personal and relational growth. The process becomes an opportunity for mutual empowerment and collaboration. Navigating through the TERMS (Twitterpated, Enlightenment, Realization, Maneuver, and Sure Love) relationship phases helps identify both partners' love languages, facilitating a more harmonious exchange of giving and receiving.

ICEBERG INSIGHTS

The iceberg is recognizing how to give and how to receive. In the different relationship phases, it might be easier to give while others want to receive. Understand the TERMS of a relationship cycle. In addition, uncovering how your partner reacts when you serve and whether your partner reciprocates is important because a one-sided relationship can cause resentment, isolation, anger, and disaster. Is there give and take, who is your partner? Identify if they are service-oriented and humble or prideful.

CHAPTER 16

Summit the Iceberg

"A healthy relationship manifests when someone embraces your history, stands by your current journey, and motivates your future aspirations."

CHARISSE WALKER

Leo has climbed Mount Rainier several times. At seventy-five years old he attempted to climb it again. He trained for several months to successfully make this ascent. In the middle of the night, he, along with his hired guides and friends, started their journey. Their goal was to reach the summit by 4:00 a.m. so they could make it back down the mountain before the snow started to melt and it got treacherous. After a few hours, one guide approached Leo and told him that he needed to return to base camp because he was too slow for the rest of the climbers. He was heartbroken and devastated. Because he was loyal to his group, trusted his guide, and was committed to everyone's success, he returned to base camp as instructed to ensure the group's safety. Although he wanted to accomplish his goal, it was not possible.

CLIMBING THE SUMMIT IS A HUGE ACCOMPLISHMENT, but sometimes the journey is just as enjoyable, and you are not supposed to reach the summit. When that happens, identify what you learned from the relationship and how you could improve the next one.

The journey to marriage is an incredible and transformative part of life. In the initial section of this book, Part I guided you through the process of confronting and overcoming personal traumas, providing tools to break through barriers and find healing. The intention was to equip you with the mental and emotional clarity needed to make healthy decisions.

Subsequently, in Part II, after achieving a sense of restoration, you embarked on a journey to acquire skills for discernment to uncover your partner's hidden iceberg. This phase emphasized the importance of looking beyond surface impressions to identify if the person you are dating is authentically revealing himself, or presenting a façade. It also encouraged you to take the time to understand your potential spouse and evaluate your compatibility. The topics covered in this section provided a trail guide to navigate the potential pitfalls and complexities of your potential spouse.

The skills and techniques you learned in this book are meant to be like items you pack into your backpack as you prepare to hike your flipped iceberg. If you are dating, I hope you took time to answer the questions and complete the activities in the accompanying workbook. Through thoughtful conversations, you have laid the groundwork for understanding, trust, and shared values, all essential for building a solid foundation for a successful marriage.

By now, you should have determined whether it is necessary to reevaluate your current situation and return to base camp and explore alternative icebergs, or persist in reaching the summit of your current relationship. If you have opted to abandon the pursuit with your current partner and return to base camp, particularly if you were in a long-term relationship, I acknowledge the difficulty of your decision and commend your courage to find a new iceberg to climb. Listening to your intuition, and redirecting your focus on a new and promising iceberg is difficult. You may have feelings of discouragement, attempting to convince you that finding the right partner is elusive. Resist the temptation to settle or remain in a relationship that does not feel right. Instead, remain active and diligent in your quest for a new iceberg.

If you recognized that there are still areas for improvement and important conversations to have with your partner, but you believe the journey up the iceberg is worth continuing, that is wonderful! Extend grace, understanding, and dedication with yourself and your partner to foster a healthy and thriving connection. Commit to working on the relationship once you feel it is the right path forward.

Much like my own experience, you may realize that the icebergs you have been eyeing are not the right fit. Be receptive to diverse and novel possibilities by overlooking the mere ten percent visible above water—dig deeper, flip the iceberg, and behold the entire mountain. This perspective shift may lead you to discover a hiking companion you might never have considered.

A word of caution: no matter how high you climb after you have flipped the iceberg, and despite your best efforts to unveil the hidden depths of your partner, sometimes the crevices are deeper than you could have ever seen. Know that you did the best you could and in these situations, it is not your fault you were deceived. If the situation is toxic or abusive, make a plan to exit the relationship as quickly as possible. Do not justify or think you can do it alone. You will emerge stronger once you break free. Trust yourself and your intuition and heed the support and advice from those around you qualified to help you.

Preparing for marriage is not about finding a definitive checklist or a foolproof guide; it is about cultivating a profound emotional connection, and committing to the ongoing journey of self-discovery and mutual growth. The conversations you have while dating are a starting point. As you get more serious, revisit these topics as you and your partner grow and adapt. Approach these conversations with empathy, respect, and a genuine desire to understand your partner's perspective. Nurture an environment of trust, where both of you feel safe expressing your thoughts, desires, and concerns.

This journey is an evolving journey, fraught with challenges, blisters, fatigue, and hunger. Embark on this beautiful, transformative journey armed with hope, patience, and an unwavering belief in the power of love. Let the insights in this book illuminate your path, encouraging you to cherish each other, embrace the challenges, and revel in the joys of a shared lifetime. If you have overcome trauma and emerged victorious, congratulations are in order—you have transformed from a victim to a victor. Embrace the opportunity to know your partner deeply, celebrating your connections. Once you reach the summit, savor the view as it is breathtaking, and the sense of accomplishment and pride is unparalleled when you find the right mate to enjoy it with.

Your love story is unique. Embrace the adventure, honor your commitment, and may your marriage be filled with love, joy, and fulfillment. I commend you for turning trauma into triumph and wish you all the best on your journey together. As you are now on the continously looped roller coaster together, embrace your commitment and enjoy the ride!

ICEBERG INSIGHTS

The overarching goal is twofold: 1) identifying your trauma and the effects it has had on your relationships so you can become triumphant over it and achieved a healthy personal well-being so you can think clearly when choosing a mate, and 2) unveiling the true nature of your potential mate to avoid entering a lasting relationship based on misconceptions.

"Flipping the Iceberg" is about revealing the unknown to pave the way for lasting happiness and a successful marriage. The dating process is a journey to uncover every aspect of the person, promoting a foundation for a happy and fulfilling relationship. Through the exercises in this book, the aim is to help you achieve enduring joy and become an example of a thriving marriage instead of one of the 50 percent that end in divorce.

Notes

1   Greenstein, Gregg. "Real Estate Divorce Specialist Training." Speech, August 9, 2021.

2   Previtera, Petrelli. "Divorce Statistics for 2022." Petrelli Previtera, LLC, January 9, 2023. https://www.petrellilaw.com/divorce-statistics-for-2022/.

3   Vuleta, Branka. "Divorce Rate in America: 35 Stunning Stats for 2023." Divorce Rate in America: 35 Stunning Stats for 2023, May 20, 2023. https://legaljobs.io/blog/divorce-rate-in-america/.

4   Livingston, Gretchen. "The Changing Profile of Unmarried Parents." Pew Research Center's Social & Demographic Trends Project, April 25, 2018. https://www.pewresearch.org/social-trends/2018/04/25/the-changing-profile-of-unmarried-parents/.

5   Livingston, "Changing Profile."

6   Mcleod, Saul. "Maslow's Hierarchy of Needs Theory." Simply Psychology, November 24, 2023. https://www.simplypsychology.org/maslow.html.

7   Weir, Kirsten. "The Lasting Impact of Neglect." Monitor on Psychology, June 14, 2014. https://www.apa.org/monitor/2014/06/neglect.

8   Kapadia, Rashmi. "What Does Your Child Learn in the Formative Years? Here Are Some Answers." The Indian Express, December 12, 2020. https://indianexpress.com/article/parenting/learning/what-does-your-child-learn-in-the-formative-years-here-are-some-answers-7100688/.

9   Weir, "Lasting Impact."

10 Mcleod, "Maslow's Hierarchy."

11 Mcleod, "Maslow's Hierarchy"

12 *The Slipper and the Rose.* United States: Universal Pictures, 1976.

13 Isa 1:18 (King James Version)

14 Anesi, Chuck. "Titanic Disaster: Official Casualty Figures and Commentary." anesi.com. Accessed December 29, 2021. https://www.anesi.com/titanic.htm.

15 Sweeney, Michael S. "Despite the Warning 'Iceberg, Right Ahead!' the Titanic Was Doomed." Culture & History, April 11, 2022. https://www.nationalgeographic.co.uk/history-and-civilisation/2022/04/despite-the-warning-iceberg-right-ahead-the-titanic-was-doomed.

16   "Iceberg Guide: How They Form, Where They're Found, and How They're Used by Wildlife." Discover Wildlife, January 11, 2021. https://www.discoverwildlife.com/holidays-days-out/antarctica/iceberg-guide/.

17   Gore, Amanda. "Finding the Joy in Life." Conference at Brian Buffini Mastermind, San Diego, CA, August 9, 2023.

18   "Brain Facts." Healthy Brains by Cleveland Clinic, May 11, 2020. https://healthybrains.org/brain-facts/.

19   Verma, Prakhar. "Destroy Negativity from Your Mind with This Simple Exercise." Medium, April 16, 2021. https://medium.com/the-mission/a-practical-hack-to-combat-negative-thoughts-in-2-minutes-or-less-cc3d1bddb3af.

20   Tandon, Abhinav, and VK Singh. "Impact of Mahatma Gandhi☒s Concepts on Mental Health: Reflections." *Indian Journal of Psychiatry* 55, no. 6 (2013): 231. https://doi.org/10.4103/0019-5545.105540.

21   Chicken Little: Hartwell, Marjorie. *Chicken little*. Racine, WI: Western Pub. Co., 1964.

22   Verma, "Destroy Negativity."

23   Santonastasso, Nick. "Master Your Internal World to Have What You Want in the External World." Conference at Multi-Family Live, Hartford, Tennessee, June 2, 2023.

24   Mashore, Krista. *Stop, Snap, and Switch: Train Your Brain to Unleash Your Limitless Life*. Las Vegas, NV, 2023.

25   Huddleston, Tom. "How Michael Jordan Became Great: 'Nobody Will Ever Work as Hard as I Work.'" CNBC, April 21, 2020. https://www.cnbc.com/2020/04/21/how-michael-jordan-became-great-nobody-will-ever-work-as-hard.html.

26   Huddleston, "How Michael Jordan."

27   Huddleston, "How Michael Jordan."

28   Cox, Daniel A, Beatrice Lee, and Dana Popsky. "Politics, sex, and sexuality: The growing gender divide in American Life." April 27, 2022. https://www.americansurveycenter.org/research/march-2022-aps/.

29   Donato, Alessandra. "Peripheral Nervous System," Queensland Brain Institute —University of Queensland, 12 July 2022. qbi.uq.edu.au/brain/brain-anatomy/peripheral-nervous-system.

30   Hendrix, Drew. "What Is Your "Gut Feeling," Anyway," inc.com, March 16, 2015. www.inc.com/drew-hendricks/what-is-your-gut-feeling-anyway.html.

31   Hendrix, "What Is Your."

32   IESE Standout. "Intuitive Decision Making. How Does It Work?" IESE

33   "Understanding Unconscious Bias." NPR, July 15, 2020. https://www.npr.org/2020/07/14/891140598/understanding-unconscious-bias.

34   Pediatrics. "How Peer Pressure Affects Teenagers." Scripps Health, September 10, 2021. http://www.scripps.orgnews_items/4648-how-does-peer-pressure-affect-a-teen-s-social-development.

35   Shetty, Jay. 8 rules of Love: How to find it, keep it, and let it go. London: Thorsons, 2023.

36   Hardy, Darren. *The compound effect: Multiplying your success, one simple step at a time.* New York, NY: Vanguard Press, 2010.

37   Burkus, David. "You are Not the Average of the Five People You Surround Yourself With." Medium, May 23, 2018. https://medium.com/the-mission/youre-not-the-average-of-the-five-people-you-surround-yourself-with-f21b-817f6e69.

38   The New Yorker. "The Iceberg: A Story by Zelda Fitzgerald." The New Yorker, December 20, 2013. http://www.newyorker.com/books/page-turner/the-iceberg-a-story-by-zelda-fitzgerald.

39   Sohn, Emily. "Turns out, Lost People Really Walk in Circles." NBCNews.com, August 20, 2009. https://www.nbcnews.com/id/wbna32494981.

40   Moran, Brendan, and Michael Lennington. *The 12 Week Year.* John Wiley & Sons, 2013.

41   Collins, Bryan. "The Pomodoro Technique Explained." Forbes, March 3, 2020. https://www.forbes.com/sites/bryancollinseurope/2020/03/03/the-pomodoro-technique/?sh=25daf16b3985.

42   Ray, Alex. "Walt Disney: It All Began with a Dream." Pioneering Minds, June 11, 2020. https://www.pioneeringminds.com/disney/.

43   Braden, Donna. "Walt Disney and His Creation of Disneyland -- the Henry Ford Blog - Blog." The Henry Ford, July 13, 2020. https://www.thehenryford.org/explore/blog/walt-disney-and-his-creation-of-disneyland.

44   "Disney Net Worth 2010-2023: DIS." Macrotrends, December 27, 2023. https://www.macrotrends.net/stocks/charts/DIS/disney/net-worth.

45   Ray, Alex. "Walt Disney: It All Began with a Dream." Pioneering Minds, June 11, 2020. https://www.pioneeringminds.com/disney/.

46   Sullivan, Dan, and Benjamin Hardy. *10x is easier than 2x: How world-class entrepreneurs achieve more by doing less.* Carlsbad, CA: Hay House Inc, 2023.

47   "Setting Daily Intentions for Positive Change." Newport Academy, May 22, 2020. https://www.newportacademy.com/resources/restoring-families/setting-daily-intentions/?utm_source=google&utm_medium=cpc&utm_campaign=NA_leads_performancemax&utm_term=&kpid=go_cmp-17884784088_adg-_ad-__dev-c_ext-_prd-&gclid=Cj0KCQjwk96lBh-DHARIsAEKO4xa2bWYLbvFHB_Q3r7XZkEA-q6s5r6RpbkNkFxgdP-mhtxjwIk9QSNwYaAgevEALw_wcB.

48   Tctn, Tony. "The story about two wolves that has shaped my life," January 23, 2019. https://tonytctn.medium.com/the-story-about-two-wolves-that-has-shaped-my-life-7fc31691a56a.

49   Bezdek, Kylie Garber, and Eva H Telzer. "Have No Fear, the Brain Is Here! How Your Brain Responds to Stress." Frontiers for Young Minds. December 20, 2017. https://kids.frontiersin.org/articles/10.3389/frym.2017.00071.

50   McKay, Brett & Kate. "The Generations of Men: How the Cycles of History Shape Your Values and Your Future." The Art of Manliness, July 1, 2023. https://www.artofmanliness.com/character/knowledge-of-men/strauss-howe-generational-cycle-theory/.

51   "Co-Dependency." Mental Health America. Accessed November 27, 2023. https://www.mhanational.org/co-dependency.

52   Kristenson, Sarah. "15 Codependent Personality Traits and Characteristics." Happier Human, January 9, 2023. https://www.happierhuman.com/codependent-traits/.

53   Ferguson, Peggy, L. "Survival Roles Develop Within the Family of Alcoholics and Addicts." http://www.peggyferguson.com/userfiles/10846/file/Survival%20Roles%20Develop%20Within%20The%20Family%20of%20Alcoholics%20and%20Addicts.pdf

54   Homestead Schools, "Codependency." https://www.homesteadschools.com/course/codependency-3/

55   Luke 23:34 (KJV)

56   McClung, Ron. "The Prayer That Lifted Martin Luther King, Jr." The Wesleyan Church, January 14, 2014. https://www.wesleyan.org/the-prayer-that-lifted-martin-luther-king-jr-1508.

57   Sandberg, Jonathan G. "Healing = Courage + Action + Grace." BYU Speeches, January 21, 2014. https://speeches.byu.edu/talks/jonathan-g-sandberg/healing-courage-action-grace/.

58   Eco Lips Store. "5 Ways to Give Yourself the Gift of Grace." Eco Lips Store. Accessed July 23, 2023. https://ecolips.com/blogs/news/5-ways-to-give-yourself-the-gift-of-grace.

59   John 8:32 (KJV)

60   Monson, Thomas S. "The Call for Courage." The Church of Jesus Christ of Latter-day Saints, April 2, 2004. https://www.churchofjesuschrist.org/study/general-conference/2004/04/the-call-for-courage?lang=en

61   Heid, Markham. (March 19, 2020). "Depression and Suicide Rates Are Rising Sharply in Young Americans, New Report Says. This May Be One Reason Why." Time. Accessed December 27, 2021 from https://time.com/5550803/depression-suicide-rates-youth/

62   Castronuovo, Celine. "CA school district's board resigns after unknowingly

talking about parents in a virtual meeting." The Hill, February 20, 2021. Retrieved from https://thehill.com/homenews/state-watch/539746-ca-school-districts-board-resigns-after-unknowingly-talking-about

63   Williams, Noah. "15 Signs You're Not Ready for Marriage." Marriage Advice - Expert Marriage Tips & Advice, April 27, 2023. https://www.marriage.com/advice/pre-marriage/10-signs-you-are-not-ready-to-get-married/.

64   Gonsalves, Kelly. "8 Signs You're Insecure in Your Relationship, from Psychologists." What It Means To Be Insecure In A Relationship, May 5, 2023. https://www.mindbodygreen.com/articles/insecure-in-relationships.

65   NG, Christina, Tess Scott, Acacia Nunes, Brian Mezerski, and Lauren Effron. "Turpin Children Describe 1st Experience Knowing They Were Free from 'House of Horrors.'" ABC7 Los Angeles, November 18, 2021. https://abc7.com/turpin-family-house-of-horrors-jordan-children/11249687/.

66   Peterson, Sarah. "Effects." The National Child Traumatic Stress Network, June 11, 2018. https://www.nctsn.org/what-is-child-trauma/trauma-types/complex-trauma/effects.

67   Lu, Wendy. "How to Deal with a Partner Who Has Baggage, Because Everyone Has Tough Stuff They're Coping With." Bustle, January 17, 2017. https://www.bustle.com/p/how-to-deal-with-a-partner-who-has-baggage-because-everyone-has-tough-stuff-theyre-coping-with-29495.

68   Taibbi L.C.S.W., Robert. "6 Reasons Why Affairs Eventually Fall Apart | Psychology Today." Psychology Today, February 16, 2020. https://www.psychologytoday.com/us/blog/fixing-families/202002/6-reasons-why-affairs-eventually-fall-apart.

69   Davenport, Barrie. "Do Affairs That Break Up a Marriage Last? Here's What You Must Know." WebMD, Aug. 12, 2022. https//www.liveboldandbloom.com/08/relationships/do-affairs-last

70   Vuleta, "Divorce Rate."

71   Stanley, Scott M, and Galena K Rhoades. "What's the Plan? Cohabitation, Engagement, and Divorce." Cohabitation Report Apr 2023, April 2023. https://ifstudies.org/ifs-admin/resources/reports/cohabitationreportapr2023-final.pdf.

72   Gen. 2:24 (KJV)

73   Munster, Rick. "5 Bad Money Habits That Can Ruin Your Relationships." Money Fit, August 11, 2022. https://www.moneyfit.org/bad-money-habits-that-ruin-relationships/.

74   Anesi, "Titanic Disaster."

75   "Equal Pay Day 2023: Department of Labor Initiatives Seek to Close Gender, Racial Wage Gap, Increase Equity in Federal Programs." DOL. Accessed July 27, 2023.https://www.dol.gov/newsroom/releases/osec/osec20230314.

76   "NCADV: National Coalition Against Domestic Violence." The Nation's Leading Grassroots Voice on Domestic Violence. Accessed October 18, 2023. https://

ncadv.org statistics?gclid=Cj0KCQjwhL6pBhDjARIsAGx8D587na524aowX-iOJLDHZK91wsbCkvpTKed9xCo7otdVDfBNuT3fwtSsaAtNeEALw_wcB.

77   "Domestic Violence Statistics." The Hotline, July 4, 2023. https://www.thehotline.org/stakeholders/domestic-violence-statistics/#:~:text=81%25%20of%20women%20who%20experienced,J.%2C%20%26%20Stevens%2C%20M.R.

78   "National Child Abuse Statistics from NCA." National Children's Alliance, August 3, 2023. https://www.nationalchildrensalliance.org/media-room/national-statistics-on-child-abuse/.

79   Nguyen, TP, Karney, BR, and Bradbury, TN. "Childhood Abuse and Later Marital Outcomes: Do Partner Characteristics Moderate the Association?" Journal of family psychology: JFP: journal of the Division of Family Psychology of the American Psychological Association (Division 43), April 11, 2016. https://pubmed.ncbi.nlm.nih.gov/27064351/.

80   Hamilton, Patrick. "Gas Light." Richmond: London, 1938.

81   Ehproject Staff. May 10, 2023. "Effective Ways To Calm Yourself Down: 6 Techniques To Find Inner Peace in 2023." E-Health Project. Retrieved on July 27, 2023 from https://www.ehproject.org/mental-health/how-to-calm-down.#:~:text=How%20long%20does%20it%20take,body%20to%20physiologically

82   US Department of Commerce, National Oceanic and Atmospheric Administration. "What Is an Iceberg?" NOAA's National Ocean Service, February 1, 2009. https://oceanservice.noaa.gov/facts/iceberg.html.

83   "Iceberg Guide: How They Form, Where They're Found, and How They're Used by Wildlife." Discover Wildlife, January 11, 2021. https://www.discoverwildlife.com/holidays-days-out/antarctica/iceberg-guide/.

84   Davidson, Sloane. "What You Give You Will Get Back Tenfold." Cosmopolitan, September 25, 2009. https://www.thecausemopolitan.com/what-you-give-you-will-get-back-tenfold.

85   Acts 20:35 (KJV)

86   Tew, Robert. "30 Days of Carrying My Wife - Live Life Happy Story." Live Life Happy, July 14, 2015. https://livelifehappy.com/stories/30-days-of-carrying-my-wife/.

87   Chapman, Gary D. The 5 love languages: Singles edition. Chicago, IL: Northfield Publishing, 2017.

About the Author

CHARISSE WALKER is a powerhouse coach and businesswoman with a unique perspective on life and relationships. With a master's degree in business under her belt, she swiftly rose to leadership in proprietary education, teaching college at the age of twenty-two and directing colleges by thirty. Her entrepreneurial spirit led her to open a college in her city before transitioning to become a Top 500 Realtor in her state and successfully running a real estate business. After a fifteen-year marriage ended painfully, leaving her a single mom of four children and subsequently losing her job, Charisse faced a pivotal turning point. This marked the beginning of her journey of self-discovery, ultimately leading her to support entrepreneurs, couples, and individuals navigating the challenges of divorce. As the host of the podcast Unbreakable Mompreneurs, Charisse shares her insights and experiences to inspire others.

Through her signature step-by-step process called Finding Hope, Charisse empowers her clients to confront their fears and uncertainties head-on, uncovering their true potential and living the life they have always dreamed of. She is driven by a mission to empower couples to create lasting marriages and help divorcees to heal from their trauma, discover their passions, and achieve their dreams through self-awareness and attaining joy.

Connect with Charisse and join her mission to create lasting change in your life and the lives of others. Visit her website, tune in to her podcast, or follow her on social media for valuable tips and inspiration.

For coaching, interviews, or speaking opportunities,
visit www.charissewalker.com
Get Free Training at flippingtheiceberg.com
Email: flippingtheiceberg@gmail.com